The Soul's Ministrations

The Soul's Ministrations   An Imaginal Journey through Crisis   •

Marianne Tauber

Chiron Publications   Wilmette, Illinois

Book and cover design by Imaginary Office.
Printed in Singapore.

ISBN 978-1-888602-54-8
Library of Congress Cataloging-in-Publication Data

Tauber, Marianne.
  The soul's ministrations : an imaginal journey through crisis / Marianne Tauber.
     p. cm.
  Includes bibliographical references and index.
  ISBN 978-1-888602-54-8
1. Active imagination. 2. Jungian psychology. I. Title.

  BF408.T268 2012
  155.9'3--dc23

                          2011031555

Contents

Introduction

It may be that, in times of crisis, the veil separating this tangible world from the invisible Otherworld is thinner, or even becomes transparent—at least for those who look "with the little eye of the soul," as the alchemist Michael Maier puts it.[1] So it was for me, in 1984, when my husband was diagnosed with a life-threatening illness that required an immediate operation, and our family was thrown into an acute crisis situation. At that time, I became engaged in an imaginal process, after stumbling upon a particular technique of painting that allowed the archetypal psyche to express itself through symbolic imagery. From its inception, this meditative exercise instilled much needed emotional strength and a deeply experienced solace. The process came to a halt naturally at the end of the immediate recovery phase. I found myself transformed, with a new perspective toward myself and life.

The body of artwork thus created never lost its meaning for me. I intuitively knew that the seventeen paintings with their assorted poems not only had negotiated a difficult passage in my life, but that they seemed to contain the promise of an ongoing enfoldment in the psyche, and, moreover, they appeared to have meaning beyond my personal attachment. Therefore, I kept them in a folder like a secret treasure, more special to me than any of my numerous dream journals. Every once in a while I showed them to a friend, and twice I presented them to a group of psychology students. On these occasions I witnessed a strong response to the images: people were touched, and their own imaginations were stimulated by what they saw.

The urge awoke to embed my artwork in a narrative that would convey the reciprocity, and often synchronicity, between my meditative activity and the course of events, as I had experienced them—to give a sense of the psychic field wherein our labile selves had been suspended at the time of crisis. Quite unexpectedly, given the many years of therapy and Jungian analysis following my husband's death in November 1989, writing the story turned into another emotional catharsis. The narrative became a kind of "healing fiction" (Hillman 1983), subjective and poetic, relying on memories, diaries, and notes—mine and those of my three children, now grown. It may have been a necessary *rite d'entrée* to my exploration of the artwork's archetypal symbolic content. The fruit of this endeavor is contained in the commentaries.

During my research, Shaun McNiff's *Art as Medicine* became an important resource. I found his own process and his insights strongly resonating with my experience at the time of crisis, as with the following observation:

Whenever illness is associated with loss of soul, the arts emerge spontaneously as remedies, soul medicine. Pairing art and medicine stimulates the creation of a discipline through which imagination treats itself and recycles its vitality back to daily living. (1992, p. 1)

Art as medicine, he continues, is "the soul's instinctual process of ministering to itself," a formulation that inspired the title for my book. Evidently, at the sudden onset of my husband's illness I incurred a momentary, but profound, *loss of soul*. My paintings, then, became a way of *soul-making* through which I was able to retrieve, little by little, what had been lost, and integrate it in a new way.[2]

I have come to regard my work as one of the many examples of C. G. Jung's "active imagination."[3] As he describes it, there are two basic parts to the process: The first is to let the unconscious psyche express itself through a creative means, such as "dramatic, dialectic, visual, acoustic, or in the form of dancing, painting, drawing, or modeling" (1954a, par. 400). The second is to seek understanding of what has transpired.[4] Concerning the first part of the process, Jung wisely remarked that "often the hands know how to solve a riddle with which the intellect has wrestled in vain" (1955–56, par. 180). This was true for me, although mine was not a case of intellectual wrestling, but rather one of mental paralysis in which no thoughts, words, or even images would come to my rescue. I found myself sitting in the abyss, the void. Moreover, I never intended to create a series when I made that first painting. But once it was done and I had responded with a poem, a vital connection to the psyche was reestablished, and the process seemingly came alive with its own momentum. I was simply drawn irresistibly to create the next painting, and then the next—a servant to the invisible, inner force. Jung considered such series of archetypal images a testimony of the objective psyche's apparently innate aim at individuation (1958, par. 576).

My interest in revisiting the artwork was to research the archetypal symbolic content present in the images—the transpersonal aspect beyond the "medicinal" quality they had for me at the time of creation. I am fond of Jung's felicitous use of the German word *betrachten*, which, in its root sense, means "making pregnant":

And if it is pregnant, then something is due to come out of it; it is alive, it produces, it multiplies. That is the case with any fantasy image; one concentrates upon it, and then finds that . . . it gets restless, it shifts, something is added, or it multiplies itself; one fills it with living power and it becomes pregnant. (1939–1941, vol. 2, p. xx)

And so I have watched my paintings and poems become pregnant with meaning in a new way, this time, in addition to sitting with them in contemplation, by drawing from literature and dictionaries as I saw fit. I have considered each painting and the accompanying poem as a unit. The poems, which came as an immediate response to the images, reveal the feelings and thought processes at the moment of creation but are also in themselves artistic expressions replete with metaphors from the storehouse of the personal, cultural, and collective unconscious.

In retrospect, I am now in a position to view the series of images and poems as a whole body, anticipating the development from the first tentative painting to the jubilant culmination of the last. My personal journey since has taken me to a place where I have come to view the figure in the last painting as a spontaneous representation of the once upon a time and, by all accounts, reemerging archetype of the goddess. I think that part of the numinous power my paintings have exerted since their creation might be her secret calling. The awareness has set me on my path: to re-search and trace her "footsteps" possibly hiding in the symbolism of the pictures that lead to her revelation in the last one. Given pertaining literature, my own experiences, and being with women in my practice, I am aware of the deep (and often deeply unconscious) desire in women to be mirrored by the archetypal divine feminine, in all possible aspects. In Christine Downing's words, "we are *starved for images* which recognize the sacredness of the feminine and the complexity, richness, and nurturing power of female energy" (1969, p. 4; emphasis added). In these efforts, the work and writings of the archaeologist Marija Gimbutas, in her seminal book *The Language of the Goddess* (1989), has been an invaluable guide. Christine Downing sees meaning in talking about *the* goddess: "To appreciate the significance of the more highly differentiated images of feminine divinity . . . , we must first understand the richness of the primitive (primary) background out of which they emerge" (1969, p. 7). This seems to be especially pertinent to the situation underlying the artwork, which represents a metaphorical life-death-rebirth cycle, evoking foremost this primary, archaic goddess who once was in charge of these processes. Speaking of *the* goddess may also be an abstraction quite possibly arising "from a longing for a feminine divinity equal in power and significance to the god of patriarchal monotheism" (ibid., p. 24). Perhaps contemporary women need to acknowledge the longing for an omnipotent female divinity initially, and perhaps as initiation, in order to feel empowered.

When I revisited the paintings, I was surprised to find that the archetypal divine masculine had been constellated as well, and from the very beginning. In a parallel process to that of the goddess, it developed from a hidden and unrecognized presence to a triumphant birth. In this respect, I valued Robert Bly's account, *Iron John: A Book about Men* (1990). At once researched and poetic, it traces the development of the divine masculine from its prehistoric beginnings to modern times.

Women writers on the goddess and feminist Jungian authors have pointed out that much of the early work on the ancient goddess traditions was carried out by men, among them Johann Jakob Bachofen (*Mutterrecht und Urreligion,* 1861; see Manheim 1967), C. G. Jung (*Symbols of Transformation,* 1952c) and Erich Neumann (*The Great Mother,* 1955). One exception is Esther Harding, who wrote *Women's Mysteries, Ancient and Modern* (1935), which was a revelation in her time and is still considered a valid resource these days. Notwithstanding the valuable feminist critique, I have found myself draw-ing extensively from these works for amplification—Neumann's in particular, because it contains so much detailed information, including a wonder-ful collection of pictures, and because it is inspired by a feeling of rever-ence and awe. Barbara Walker's *The Women's Encyclopedia of Myths and Secrets* (1983) has been a steady companion throughout, and Chevalier and Gheerbrant (1969) was my most frequently consulted dictionary of symbols.

Reading Jung's writings on active imagination has quite naturally sparked my interest in alchemy, for Jung frequently referred to the parallel between the symbolism contained in the work of historic medieval alchemy, his process of active imagination, and the depth-psychological development he called individuation.[5] As my main guide into the alchemical symbolism I have relied foremost on volumes 12, 13, and 14 of Jung's *Collected Works,* which specifi-cally concern themselves with alchemy, enriched by Edward Edinger's orga-nizing and enlightening *Anatomy of the Psyche* (1985). Jim Henderson and Dyane Sherwood's delightful *Transformation of the Psyche* (2003) and Stanton Marlan's intense work *The Black Sun* (2005), as well as the diverse writings on alchemy (now collected in one volume in the handsome uniform edition) by James Hillman (2010), have provided valuable insight. In addition, I often consulted Abraham's *Dictionary of Alchemical Imagery* (1998). My choices for the amplification in both fields of inquiry—archetypal symbolism and alchemi-cal psychology—are but impressionistic brushstrokes, but, standing back, I find that they have come together to create three-dimensional pictures that have come alive in a new way.

Autobiographical Notes

Although I found myself in a void at the time of crisis, the discovery of my kind of meditative (or, as I will call it, "alchemical") painting did not come out of nothing. Since we had known each other, my husband and I had tended to our dreams, sharing and interpreting them and giving them artistic form through painting, clay, wood carvings, and music, even amplifying them through Jung's method of active imagination, and this activity had laid the foundation. These had been practices modeled by my husband's parents, my in-laws, who remained our most enthusiastic mentors—before and after our immigration to the United States.

I was born and raised in Zürich as the oldest daughter of highly cultured and very busy physicians. Claire Douglas (1990) captures Switzerland well with regard to the late nineteenth-century background to Jung's psychology, which still held true for the mid-twentieth: the landscape with its "Romantic geography" (p. 21), contrasting with its people, whose Swiss character is perceived as sober, pragmatic, and almost restricted. Sociopolitically, as Douglas describes it, Switzerland was a respectable patriarchy (and Zürich stoutly Protestant, I might add), with its attitude toward women both underhandedly misogynistic and idealistically romantic.

In 1962, my family moved from Zürich to Winterthur. I was barely an adult and freshly enrolled at the University of Zürich after a year abroad. Soon, we were invited by the Taubers for dinner, and I distinctly remember the evening. I felt a mystery pervading their house that I could not put my finger on: the creaking of the old wooden staircase to the second floor (a practice occupied the first) as if telling stories of olden times, family portraits and strange, gnarly wooden sculptures looking down at us, and a secret seeming to loom around every dark corner. We were crowded around the large round dinner table; our elbows touched each other and almost touched the bookshelves lining the walls around us and extending into a music and study room on one side and a sitting room on the other. The parents reminisced about their years in medical school in Zürich, while the children (four of the five Taubers and three in my family) eyed each other with curiosity and exchanged pleasantries. Soon, however, the conversation turned to Dr. Jung, who had been an immeasurable influence in the Taubers' lives and whose death they were still mourning.[6]

I listened, mesmerized, while they shared memories of their experiences with the revered "wise old man." Worlds upon worlds were opening before me of which I had known nothing while growing up—that there was meaning to our nightly dreams and their importance for a symbolic attitude toward life, that fairy tales and myths and even religion could be interpreted psychologically. Furthermore, astrology and Zen Buddhism ("the culture of stillness," as introduced by Karlfried Graf Dürckheim to the West) were brought into the conversation. As a consequence, I began to record my dreams in a journal and frequently sought counsel from the Taubers and their eldest son Jürg.

Eventually, Jürg and I entered the bond for life. As my father-in-law observed, tongue in cheek, our marriage was "destiny," as our family had moved to Schickstrasse, while they lived on Salstrasse—and *Schicksal* means fate or destiny in German. Emulating my revered mother-in-law, I left my studies at the University of Zürich to devote myself, as she had done, to being a wife, mother, and homemaker—although I pursued a modest career as a classical singer.

Jürg, an aspiring surgeon, soon moved his young family from Zürich to Bern and, from there, to New York City, with a grant to join the liver transplant team at the Sloan-Kettering Memorial Hospital. When he became frustrated by the vexing problems the team faced in transplant rejections, he decided to returned to school to earn a PhD in immunology at the Rockefeller University, in order to conduct basic research. These were our student years, in which we were poor but relatively happy and carefree. We subsisted in a tiny apartment on First Avenue with our two, then three children, without television, but with live music and silent meditation instead. The Zen Studies Society, the Jung Institute, and the Dalcroze School of Music were our havens. Jürg underwent analysis with Edward Edinger.

After receiving his PhD, Jürg was promoted to assistant professor in immunology, and we were able to move into an apartment on the top floor of the newly constructed faculty building. A few years later, however, he felt the need to undertake an American surgical residency, which would allow him to work as a surgeon in the U.S. and personally execute the experiments he had designed to support insights gained in his research. We moved to Chicago, where Jürg was accepted into the residency program at the University of Illinois, which included the Cook County and Veterans' Administration hospitals. Those four years turned out to be a most grueling—and, for me, a most worrisome—period in Jürg's career and a strain on our family life. After a somewhat easier fellowship in transplant surgery at the University of Chicago, he had finally arrived, having single-mindedly followed the star of his destiny—until fate, so it seemed, caught up with him . . . and this is where my story begins.

Narrative

Tuesday, 15 May

Softly promising daylight greeted me as I opened my eyes. Everything was in its normal place, peaceful, quiet, and friendly. It was a beautiful morning in May. The cheerful sounds of bird voices and the delicate fragrances of flowers and blossoming trees came through the open windows. For a while I just lay still, blinking my eyelids, surprised to find my body intact and the house still standing in its normal place. It must have been a dream then, this strange, frightening experience of being sucked up into a gray void, whirled around with everything else that flew into the air: the house, its contents, the trees, the garage, other people.

We were sleeping in the den at the time. Jürg, already sitting at his low desk under the window, Zen style, noticed me waking up and turned around to greet me. But a look at my puzzled face made him ask, instead, "What's up?" So, still a bit numbed, I told him my dream. It appeared to make a deep impression on him. If I had expected some sort of joking remark about my "weird kind of nirvana," it did not happen; instead, he sat there, strangely moved, fighting to control his emotions. Finally he murmured something about a time approaching when things might feel just like in that dream, ". . . so maybe you are being prepared."

He motioned me to sit down beside him, pulling out his dream journal and hesitantly opening it. The morning had turned unnaturally still as I waited with rising expectation to hear, or see, what he would reveal to me. On the page was a painting—but what did it represent, this big, black blot with some pink? After a long pause, my husband gently told me that he had recently seen "this woman" in a dream. She was called "The Naked Truth." He was in no hurry to say more, so we just sat there, staring at the picture in silence.

Upon looking closely, I could discern the shape of a woman, crouched on the floor, her knees pulled to her chest, her long black hair falling over her body. She seemed slightly bent over, perhaps weighed down by her hair. Or perhaps she was sad, infinitely sad. A silent, faceless presence of quiet power and simplicity, she impressed me as someone strangely ancient and foreign, but also deeply familiar in her womanhood. She touched me at the core of my being. This woman called "The Naked Truth" made an impression on me as if she would not let herself be manipulated into any scheme of work, studies, goals, plans, or ideals, and she seemed to forbid any sort of smart interpretation. She was not to be analyzed; there was nothing to be associated or amplified, and no sophisticated conclusion about her was to be extracted. She came from a place deeper and more basic, a woman's mysterious place of intimate connection to earth and bodily existence. By the same token, her long black hair, her posture, and her unmistakable name conveyed something sinister and urgent.

Finally, taking a deep breath and choosing his words carefully, my husband confessed what had been lying like a heavy stone on his heart for the past week: how he had not been feeling well lately or, more correctly, was suddenly feeling worse than he had over the past year. Denying it to himself, he had not taken any action until this dream prompted him to see the neurologist, a colleague at the hospital. Perhaps there was something more, after all, to a condition that had been diagnosed a few years back as "benign vertigo."

I was holding my breath with the ominous sense that something terrible would be revealed to me. Here I was, in the presence of my invincible hero whose journey I had accompanied all these years, from Zürich to Bern in our native Switzerland, from there across the ocean to the New World—New York, Chicago. A seemingly interminable period of earning degrees and enduring surgical residencies was coming to an end, and the beginning of a brilliant career was in sight. But this moment suddenly had a very different flavor— and not one of victory. What was it, exactly?

My husband's voice was coming as if from a distance, and what he said sounded unreal: the neurologist, just by looking at him, had suggested the possibility of a brain tumor. The diagnosis was confirmed after a scan: a tumor in the brain stem. At this point, operation had become a matter of urgency. With a weary smile, pointing with his chin toward the window behind his desk, Jürg added: "So that's what it was all about," hinting at some hidden meaning that just had been revealed. We both stared at the upper left corner of the window. In mysteriously synchronistic timing, a swarm of wasps had chosen that spot above Jürg's desk to build their large, cone-shaped nest hanging under the top of the frame. For months we had observed with fascination their relentless activity, which we could watch from within through the glass. Now it seemed obvious that their nest was a perfect symbol for a growth, such as a tumor.

The silence was palpable. We were sitting next to each other, absorbed in our own thoughts. Yet, in some strange way, it felt special to me to sit together in this humble demeanor. The sadness was soft and warm, with the dark presence of the woman from his dream between us. It was so unusual for us to just sit there and be together without a purpose or a goal in mind. Usually for us, "just sitting" implied Zen meditation as a joint spiritual practice, with its particular physical posture, frame of time and mind. Conversely, if the issue had been one of dealing with those caprices of the anima—bad moods and unpleasant feelings—Jürg had had many years of training in taking care of them immediately. Hundreds of poems, paintings, wood carvings, clay figures, and hours of practicing music originated in the endeavor to appease her, satisfy her needs as he perceived them. A similar regimen had been imposed on me for dealing with my animus, lest he should revolt. Alas, both anima and wife had been rather tightly controlled under my husband's yoke, harnessed to support the hero on his arduous journey.

Now we sat there without form or will to shape the world. We were facing the inevitable, numbed and stunned by the equally awesome and awful impact of fate speaking through the body. We were making room for the woman called "The Naked Truth."

Beyond my understanding, though, I felt a deep kinship to her, a secret bond, as if she had finally come to be on my side in our marriage. Fate had intervened in my husband's relentless pursuit of his destined career—a pursuit that had often left me breathless and worn out. But that morning I felt contained and content, in spite of being well aware that the consequences were unknown and potentially dreadful.

At last the house awakened with the sounds of different voices, playful laughter, the tuning of instruments. It so happened that my mother, my sister, and her two daughters were visiting from Switzerland, and this was the last day of what had been a marvelous time together. Why had Jürg waited for the last day of the visit to break the news? And, for that matter, why had he not confided in me, his wife? I never asked these questions and will never know. I suspect that he simply did not have it in him to "spoil" our family vacation and that he was holding out until the last moment.

Like a landscape suddenly darkened by clouds covering up the sun, so these tidings spread a gloomy hue over the family. In spite of his unemotional, matter-of-fact presentation, Jürg's revelation turned our Easter celebration with its farewell dinner into a day of mourning. Even the first bunch of Jürg's homegrown asparagus, to be proudly served for this special meal, took on a darkly twisted archetypal meaning. "Phallic symbols of masculinity, all cut down," he murmured, as we washed and cooked them in the kitchen.

Wednesday, 16 May

Our relatives packed their many suitcases, and I drove them to O'Hare International Airport. Everybody was in a state of shock. My mind was functioning on autopilot, but my heart was heavy with disbelief that they were going to leave me behind, "in exile." Reasonably, of course, they were going to inform Jürg's parents and together devise a rescue plan. Even so, their leaving tugged at my roots in the native soil of Switzerland. I would have to face the approaching ordeal of Jürg's illness alone.

The departure of my mother, sister, and nieces left a terrible void in the house. I wanted to sit down in the middle of the bare floor and weep—weep all the tears withheld over the many years since our emigration. I wanted to wail and keen and have everyone in the family join me. But this was out of the question; my husband would not (and perhaps could not) tolerate such a "sentimental scene." Instead, it was left to me to cook dinner. I dealt as quietly as I could with pots and pans, so as to overhear my husband's conversation with our children. I listened to him instruct them in a loving and disciplined manner about what to expect and how they would have to behave in the coming week, masterfully downplaying the unforeseeable consequences of the operation. Explaining how he had trained them well to be "peaceful warriors," whether on the aikido mats, on horseback, or generally in life, he expected them to handle this difficult situation just fine; they were to behave as though nothing out of the ordinary was happening. Dad would simply be gone for a while and then, it was to be hoped, return with a scar on his head. My eyes blurred with tears. Unable to hold them back, I helplessly (yet with a secret satisfaction) watched them drip into the spaghetti water, thinking that this would be the only acceptable way I could share my tears with my family.

I don't think anybody asked our children, at the time, how they were feeling. Only in retrospect, piecing together the story and pondering the events while writing, did I wonder what their individual experiences had been. When I asked them about it, I found their reactions and memories as different as their personalities.

Our younger daughter, who had been nine years old at the time, needed gentle prodding to open up, careful, as she always was, not to upset her mother. Finally she revealed how afraid she had been, in spite of Dad's instructions. She told me how she could not sleep that night, and when our dog Prince had come into her room, she had gotten out of bed and stayed up with him all night, praying. "In the morning I was very tired and disappointed when I was told that the operation would only be the next day, because I knew that I could not manage another sleepless night in prayer." Our older daughter, then fourteen, flatly refused to warm up old touchy stories: "If you want to know, you can dig up my journals, and you are welcome to read in them whatever you want." When I asked our son, sixteen at the time, he gravely shook his head: "I don't know, Mom; I have no memory at all. But I do remember when Dad came back—that's when things started to get crazy."

Thursday, 17 May

The moment of my husband's admittance to the hospital arrived, only two days after the news had been divulged. Jürg packed a small suitcase; there would not be much he needed or had use for. I don't remember exchanging many words on the way to the University of Chicago hospital. The eerie, almost inconceivable thought that he was going to be a patient loomed between us—that he would be one of many cases in the same hospital where he had been working as a surgeon.

Had I expected any special treatment as a result of his position, I was to be disappointed. In the receiving station, nobody even recognized him, and nobody cared. I had a hard time taming my impatience while assisting my husband with the extensive admissions paperwork—surely, they must have had it all on file. Minutes after we handed the forms back to the receptionist, two unfamiliar residents appeared, calling out Jürg's name, then politely allowing for a brief goodbye before they turned around, taking him between them. I watched them approach a double door. Jürg looked small between the two white-coated physicians, but, as I noticed with a pang in my heart, he quite obviously made a special effort to assume a professional demeanor among colleagues. The door opened to let the three men walk through and then closed swiftly behind them, panels of milky glass diffusing the view into the mysterious world on the other side. Gone . . . and I was not allowed to follow and be at his side and hold his hand during whatever preparatory procedures they had scheduled. Meekly, feeling like a little mouse lost in endless tunnels of a burrow not her own, I made my way through the corridors and at last stepped out into the bright daylight. After finding my car, I sat behind the wheel as if in a vacuum, unable to move a muscle in my body. Familiar feelings of loneliness and abandonment welled up within me.

That evening, in an angst-ridden effort to do my part, I tried especially hard to get everything ready according to our standards, a demanding combination of Swiss cleanliness and Zen serenity. Besides, there was my worry about our children, as they would have to manage on their own the next day and night. Were they going to be "okay"? Were they provided with all the

12

necessities? Would the older two be responsible and help the little one with her homework? Most important, how could we reach each other (in those times before cell phones)?

When all was taken care of and each child tucked away in bed, I withdrew to our own bedroom. Its spaciousness yawned around me as I settled on the large, empty carpet before the row of windows, each framing a square blackness. I lit a candle and listened into the silence, feeling numb and exhausted. After a long while, I reached for paint and paper in an attempt to express what I was experiencing through art, as I had done so many times before. But there was no impulse. There was nothing, really, to be painted—no object, no scene or image, nor a feeling, in the way there always was with dreams. I was staring into the void. The great void. Wondering how one could paint "nothingness," I remembered our Zen master. Of course, he would do it with one ingenious brushstroke. But not I . . . that did not fit me, and I was not about to imitate him.

Finally I dipped my big brush into the water and then soaked it with paint. Any color; it did not matter. I let the brush glide aimlessly over the paper, without attempting shape or form. Adding more paint with different colors, I watched dispassionately how they flowed into each other where they met. "Ugly," I observed, disgusted, "and meaningless." Since the paper was too wet to crumple up into a ball, I folded it in two, so that I would no longer have to look at it, rubbing the two halves together with my fist. Nothing, it seemed, was going to come to my rescue that night.

But after sitting there in stupefied heaviness for some time, a tiny spark of curiosity led my hands back to the discarded paper, carefully opening it up again. I stared at it with a sudden impulse of remembrance. Of course, this was what we often did for fun as children, and with our own children: if handled that way, the paint would dry into a curious symmetrical pattern of textured shapes and colors. Although I could not revive the sense of fun, there was an unexpected pulse of life quickening my senses. I picked up a finer brush in a sudden desire to outline and enhance the shapes I perceived, while simultaneously intuiting the emerging meaning. After the silent dialogue between the painting and my inner world subsided and nothing else needed to be added, I put the brush down in deep contemplation. Still with suspended curiosity, I noticed words arising within me, words that responded to the painting and expressed the meaning arising from within. I scrambled for a pen and another piece of paper. Almost by themselves, the words formed a poem.

As I had so often witnessed during Zen retreats, when meditation becomes more focused and the silence deepens, there comes the distinct moment when physical discomfort, emotional pain, and the clamorous mind are transcended and another reality opens up, that of "sacred space." Inadvertently, it had arrived while I had concentrated on the painting. I let my hands sink into my lap, breathing deeply and freely. I felt relief, surrounded by a benevolent, numinous presence, or perhaps presences. It was as if the yawning, gaping void had been filled with love, and I had an almost physical sense of being cradled. Thus contained and contented, I crawled into bed, extending my thoughts of peace to the hospital where, somewhere, my husband was lying in a bed.

Alas, Jürg must have endured a seemingly endless night of excruciating suffering. I only learned days later that, shortly after being admitted, he had suddenly stopped breathing and was intubated at once. A note he wrote to the nurse during that night was somehow preserved and traveled with his other belongings to the intensive care unit. But only I could fully appreciate what this heroic man must have gone through before he wrote down such an outcry of despair: "This is enough—I can't take this any more!"

Schwarzer Regenbogen senkt sich ins Meer . . .
Jetzt aber trinke den blutigen Kelch, Tiefversunkener!
Neues will wachsen,
ungeahnt, schön.

Black rainbow, sinking into the ocean . . . / Now drink the bloody cup, /
You, who dwells in unfathomable depths! / New life wants to sprout, /
beautiful, unknown.

Friday, 18 May

The day of the operation had arrived. I woke up restored, still filled with the trust the painting had bestowed on me and able to prepare my children for school and for what they would have to accomplish afterward by themselves that evening and through the night.

To my surprise, I was given a very friendly welcome at the hospital. The surgeon was personally concerned for my comfort and offered me his private office for the duration of the operation. I gratefully accepted the little haven, knowing that I would not leave it before the operation was over. I was going to focus all my energies, my mind, and my prayers on the operation, equipped with only my Zen pillow, my painting utensils, and what little else I needed for immediate survival.

The operation lasted from early morning into the afternoon. I stayed put, spending the time seated on the carpeted floor meditating and painting, with only brief intervals for stretching or bathroom breaks. Once in a while a nurse with a friendly face appeared, giving me an update on the status of the proceedings or handing me a tray with food. Sometimes her face expressed concern about me, puzzled by my behavior. But she was respectful of my needs, for which I silently thanked her. I completed two paintings during that time.

With the first one, I allowed myself to express my anger at the tumor with splashes of red and orange colors—there . . . there. As before, I folded the paper through the middle and waited for the paint to dry. Opening it up, I immediately saw the devil between two people, which of course became a symbol for the tumor that had inserted itself between us. Only minimal input was necessary to bring out the features of the image: the devil smiling mischievously and the couple, apparently in stunned silence, connected by a thin thread. Intuitively, I felt the need to address this devil in English, as if that was the one language he would understand.

The second painting, which came hours later, was no longer an expression of outrage, and the poem was less grandiose in its wording. I had come to a place of humble acceptance, of surrender. Moreover, I was immensely tired.

At long last I was told that they were "closing up" and that the surgeon would visit with me when it was all done. He was a kind, fatherly man with a humble attitude, looking terribly worn himself when he arrived—understandably, after the many hours of concentrated effort. He told me that they had found "a low-grade astrocytoma in the fourth ventricle of the brain stem," which, he said, was lucky. Although they had to leave the floor of the tumor in place, for fear of hurting vital tissue, the chances of new growth were extremely small—it might be quiet for the next thirty years. My husband would recover all right, and I was now allowed to go see him in the ICU. With a deep breath of relief, I thanked him.

With stiff and hurting legs I followed the nurse who guided me through a maze of hallways to the ICU. I was in a light trance, and stepping into the brooding, windowless ICU only enhanced the sense of otherworldliness. They left me standing beside a bed with a patient in deep coma. I stared at the hugely bandaged head, the tubes coming out of nose and mouth, sealed off with tape, the wires attached to the chest that were leading to the beeping and hissing machinery behind the bed. Various plastic tubes connected the veins in the seemingly lifeless arms, lying exposed on either side of the body, with plastic bags hanging beside the bed. My husband? Not sure—it could be anybody. After a while I left, subdued. Although still in shock, I was able to find my way to the home of Jürg's boss in the department of transplantation, not too far from the hospital, where his wife had offered me a guest room. How grateful was I for the warm welcome, food, fresh linen, a Valium, and, most importantly, a phone to get in touch with our children. Soon I was sucked up into gray oblivion.

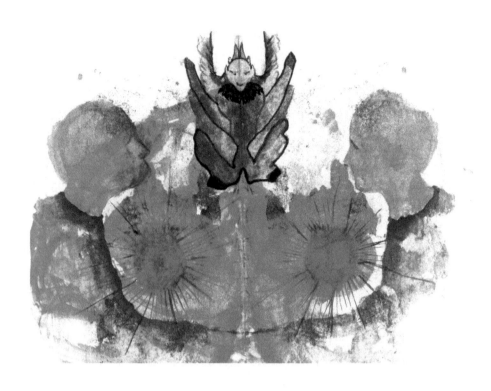

Tumor!
All your rumor
take away—end!
No more
evil, hurt . . .
But oh, we bend
to the message you send, devil:
You obey the same Great Law on the way.
So then shrink, fade away,
leave nothing back:
no vertigo, no track, no tremor.

Blauer Regenbogen steigt auf.
Ich betrachte die Vergangenheit
und schaue nach Zukünftigem;
er schlägt die Brücke.
Was unten war, wird oben sein,
und was vorne hinten.
Goldene Sonne leuchtet aus der Zukunft.

Blue rainbow rising. / I'm pondering the past / and look out for what comes. /
The rainbow throws a bridge across. / What is below will be above, /
and what in front, behind. / A golden sun is shining from the future.

Saturday, 19 May

It took a moment the following morning to recall my memories, but when they appeared I felt an overwhelming desire to vanish back into the void. Eventually I got up and found my way into the kitchen, where a lovely breakfast was waiting for me. I found that I could function surprisingly well, even though my spirit was in another world. I ate, had a conversation with my sympathetic hostess, and then walked back to the hospital.

When I returned to the ICU, my heart leaped suddenly when I saw that Jürg had come back to this world. Our eyes met in a silent gaze of recognition. I grabbed his hand and held it tenderly. It was limp and lifeless. I visualized healing energy streaming into his body through my hands while I talked, saying whatever came to mind. Jürg seemed to listen intently, soaking up the words like a thirsting wanderer who had found some droplets of water along the path. But he soon drifted off, apparently exhausted, and his eyelids closed irresistibly.

I sat by the bed and became more aware of the surroundings. A small unit, about five beds. The nurse at the next bed periodically shouted into her patient's ear: "Donald, Donald . . . can you hear me? What day is it today?" It was a futile effort, for there was never so much as a stir, let alone an answer. It annoyed me, but it was also the only way to keep me awake, and perhaps the nurse too. The warm and stagnant air made me drowsy, and the hissing, pumping, spitting sounds that emanated from various life-support machines in endlessly repetitive rhythms had a trance-inducing effect. Finally, I took the alto bamboo flute I had brought along out of its case and played a few tones, shy at first, but as nobody seemed to mind, with increasing confidence and pleasure. I improvised Zen style, letting the lonely voice of living sound penetrate the rhythms of the stereotyped, idiotic mechanical noises, knowing that somehow it would reach and touch my husband's soul.

I have no recollection of how I made my way home or in what condition I found my children. While spending the evening together, we must have talked about their dad, and I would have told them what I could, which wasn't all that much. But the memory of home life during those first trying days is blurred; only the paintings and poems remain as a lasting testimony.

My meditative way of painting had become a necessary practice as a daily source of regeneration. It was a relief to give expression, through flowing paint, to the chaotic fluidity of life in its liminal state of loss and unknowing. The folding and unfolding of paper filled with paint represented an act of agency and trust; the tracing of the dried textures in recognition of emerging forms and content was a subtle experience of revelation and, perhaps more important, of grounding and stabilizing. The exercise was at once a deadly serious prayer and a playful dance of soul.

That night, I was deeply moved by the unexpected appearance of the owl and the turtle. They seemed to emerge from the texture of the dried paint completely of their own accord. While putting the finishing touches to the owl, flying directly toward me and looking me straight in the eye, I was instilled with such a sense of awe that shivers ran up and down my spine. These venerable animals quite obviously came from dimensions beyond the personal sphere. They were visitors from far beyond, which is what I tried to express with my words.

Time was counted in two ways: one by the regular calendar, the other by post-operative days. Yet there was also "timeless time," flowing like a broad stream through our existence, leaving everything worldly at its margin. Owl and Turtle were messengers from this timeless time, coming to my aid as I traveled, like a messenger myself, between worlds and between times. They touched something at the core of my being, a source of trust and strength, for less than ever did I have an identity as a person or a sense of my own will.

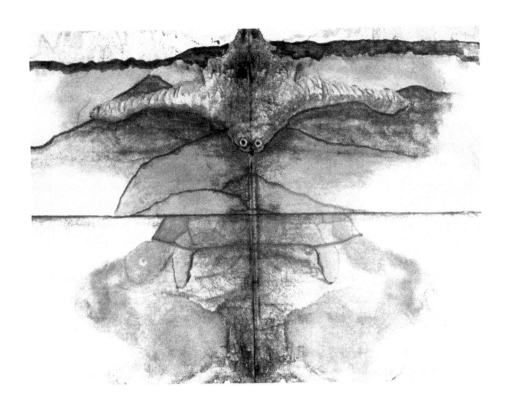

Eule!
Ich heule—
Du aber fliegst
ruhig und leicht durch die Weiten,
Längen und Breiten.
Schildkröte!
Oh grosse Nöte—
Du aber steigst
ruhig und sicher aus den Tiefen,
wo alle schliefen.

Ihr beide sind der Welten Zeichen
für Weisheit und Alter ohne Gleichen.

Owl! / I howl— / while you but soar / serenely through ether's breadths and widths. /
Turtle! / oh what pain— / but you emerge / so solemn and sure from the depths /
where they all were asleep.

You represent, for the world to see, / Wisdom and Old Age in eternity.

Sunday, 20 May

In the morning there was a brief call from my in-laws, announcing that they would arrive in a few days "to help out" and that a letter with details was on its way. I cried with utter relief and gratitude. I revered these elders like living representatives on earth of the great mother and father—yes, indeed, of wisdom and old age: Owl and Turtle had prepared me for their coming.
I decided not to go to the hospital, catching up with work at home instead. I needed a bit of distance from the hospital, to ground myself in the normal routine of daily activity and to spend some time with the children. Together we would prepare the house for our guests.

Still, there was an almost magical draw toward my secret practice, and I could not let a day go by without it. Even more than through physical presence, I felt united with my husband through the paintings I created, especially as the physical reality was still nearly unbearable: my "invincible hero" was a patient, bound up and bandaged, incapacitated, deprived of personhood. Even if conscious at times, he still was without language because of the horrible tubes obstructing his mouth and nose. I could reach him only through his eyes, and what I read in them was a deep suffering that pained me to the bones of my being. Clearly, the "palm of victory" in my painting came as a compensation for the despair I sensed in both of us.

Augenlichter werdet dichter;
konzentriert euch auf die Mitte,
wo das dritte euch vereinigt.
Wo die Siegespalme steht,
wunderbare Linderung weht,
und nichts den Liebsten peinigt.

Light of my eyes, / Densify; / Concentrate onto the middle, / where the third /
unites you both. / Where resides the victory palm, / emanating wondrous balm, /
and where nothing pains my beloved.

Monday, 21 May

The promised letter from my mother-in-law arrived. I brought it unopened to the hospital, anticipating the pleasure of reading it out loud, so we could receive the news together. Jürg, still intubated, signaled silent recognition through his eyes when I held up the envelope, watching my every move while I opened it, unfolded the pages, and cleared my throat. Upon hearing the confirmation of his parents' arrival with the exact date and time a spark lit up my husband's eyes and a subtle stream of energy seemed to move through his body, the muscles tightening and relaxing.

With inner satisfaction I was to continue eagerly, my eyes flying ahead over the page. What I gleaned, however, made me halt mid-sentence, pondering for a brief moment what to do: read what was there or pretend that it wasn't? Too late—feeling Jürg's inquiring look on my burning cheeks, I swallowed hard and decided to go on and read the sentence I had stumbled over: "We just received message that Soen Nakagawa Rōshi had died in his monastery in Japan." I took a deep sigh, letting the news sink in. Soen Rōshi had been our revered Zen master in New York, with whom Jürg had enjoyed a very special friendship, culminating when the rōshi had accepted an invitation to hold a *sesshin* in our family's little cabin on Star Mountain (*Sternenberg*) in Switzerland. But during the strenuous years of residency in Chicago we had lost contact.

Even though I expected a reaction, I was not prepared for the vehemence of Jürg's emotion. His body stiffened, eyes directed at the ceiling in a blank stare. He made an obvious effort to control himself, as he had always done. But all of a sudden his tears burst forth like a torrent, and he had to let it happen, helpless, unable to muster up the strength to hold them back and unable to utter a sound. Sitting quietly, I received those tears in silence. They came as an uncommon gift, for I could not remember ever having seen my husband cry before. As the emotion subsided, Jürg slipped into another world and was no longer present.

My painting that evening helped me digest the events of the day and transform the image I had retained in my mind of my poor husband, crazed with a pain perhaps more psychic than physical to begin with, to which the news of Soen Rōshi's death had added yet another dimension. Was it not a miracle that those plastic tubes, which inhibited Jürg from speaking, transformed into blue blossoms?

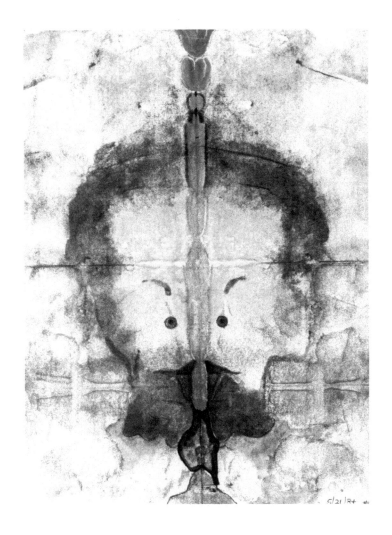

Zu später Stunde noch
entpuppt sich hier ein Mann
der wohl gut sehen kann,
doch leidet, leidet Angst und Bang.
Wann endlich kommt der Zeitpunkt doch,
wo aus dem schrecklich Vegetieren
der neue Mensch sich kann gebieren?

In the latest hour of the day / a man reveals himself / who may well see /
but suffers, suffers anxiety and pain. / When will the moment come /
when from the vegetative state / the human will be reborn?

Tuesday, 22 May

As I was to learn, a moment of synchronicity had transpired. While I had been painting late the previous night and composing my intensely felt prayer that my husband might be restored to humanity, Jürg, unsupervised, had freed himself from the tubes that connected him to the lung machine. As a surgeon, he knew the procedure well, and with enough of his old ego reawakened, he had finally grown too impatient with the hospital protocol. Of course, he shocked the staff. In his own words: "Last night I finally pulled out the tubes myself. It was very easy. It was a long time before anybody noticed, but then they were very upset."

I was surprised, too, in the morning when I discovered my husband in the more normal human condition I had wished for so ardently. At last he had his language back and could share what he had gone through since his admittance to the hospital. Not only did he wish to tell me, he wanted me to write it down in his journal, as follows:

Thursday, May 17

At about 8 a.m. they did the angiogram. I was told that it would hurt two times very much, but only for three seconds each time. I was able to withdraw from my body, and it was tolerable. The anesthesiologist was fantastic.

The rest of the day was endless. I was intubated and medicated, but I could almost not make it through the day, because I was fully present. However, I understood what they needed to do, and they did it well.

Friday, May 18

Operation. I did not remember anything about that day at all. Only today, in what seemed many months later, when my wife asked me, it suddenly all came back to me: I am in a nonhuman form that resembles somewhat a brown-black cross or a brown monk's gown of the Franciscan order, or simply a dark brown moving splash. I am not alone: there are at least six like myself—my closest friends. Soen Rōshi is among them. [At this point, he frowned and gave me a meaningful glance, reminding me of his tears.] Space, time, form, and numbers are of no importance; I am simultaneously up, talking with them outside the operation room, and lying on the operation table, but I am also standing beside it, observing the operation. The present and eternity are the same. I am myself, but also a part of my friends and of personalities of earlier epochs as well. I feel that I have known everything already, how it is, was, and how it would be. Somehow, I have lived through everything before, and I am sure glad that I do not have to do it again.

The memory of the following days is only hazy. They were endless. There was no physical pain, but the images were painful: I could not close my eyes, lest a moving mass would fall on top of me. It was a feeling of suffocating in the "magma," the earth mass. On the other hand, when I kept my eyes open, I was driven into the periphery, far, far away, and then I felt like [I was] nailed to the cross. They touch each other, those two aspects, like the two sides of an archetype.

Of this second phase, only one thing was relevant: there was no connection within the realm of experience between me and my wife. In those extreme worlds, I was alone.

He continued, now addressing me: "I should have asked without scruples for you to be at my bedside all the time. The nights were unbearable and full of anguish. Only when you were there—you and the sound of the flute—things were alright."

We sat in silent contemplation, punctuated by the rhythmic sounds of the ICU machines. The journal was resting in my lap, my hands folded on the opened pages where I had written down Jürg's entry. I was trying to absorb in my mind what I had just heard: images of monumental experiences, shared in a few simple sentences. It was perhaps due to my daily journeying into the realms of the psyche that I was able to conceive at all of such fearsome, seemingly fathomless archetypal dimensions. Still, for the extremity of his condition I had no match in my own experience. But I promised Jürg to spend the night at his bedside as soon as his parents arrived and could help out on the home front. I left with a distinct feeling of hopefulness and newfound trust.

When I returned to my painting meditation, I sank the brush deeply into the paint, mixing rich and multiple colors on the paper. As always, I kept my mind still, purposefully refraining from anticipating what would emerge. When the small mythical figure suggested itself before my inner eye, I was in awe. While I carefully outlined the unusual features of my "little prince," I felt a deep motherly love well up in my heart, and I wondered about him and spun my imaginings around him.

Aus Wasser und Feuerlichten,

aus Wolkenschichten,

steigt der Prinz empor.

Nackt ist er noch, und mager,

weil er so lange fror.

Nun will ich ihn tränken und speisen.

Er wird mir die Richtung weisen,

die er auserkor.

Er kann die Kräfte zähmen

und geht mir voran durch's Himmelstor.

Out of water and fire's blaze, / out of darkly clouded skies / emerges the prince. /
He is still naked and haggardly thin, / because he was cold for so long. /
Now I will feed him and quench his thirst. / He will point the way / which he chose. /
He will tame the powers that be / and will lead me through heaven's gate.

Wednesday, 23 May

Jürg's parents were expected to arrive in the afternoon. We were desperately looking forward to their coming, much as people in a disaster yearn for the rescue team. The guest room was ready, and the children were prepared to welcome their grandparents when they arrived from the airport. As agreed upon, I would already have returned to the hospital to spend the night with my husband. Relieved on one front, I could provide comfort on the other. How often I had played the role of the good comrade or relief worker "in battle" during those extremely strenuous years of surgical residency! Picking up an exhausted man after a 36-hour shift, nurturing him back to normal for a night and a day only to let him go again for yet another shift, had become a seemingly interminable routine, until . . . even his body evidently had reached its limits.

While such thoughts went through my head, I gathered the bare necessities: a foam pad and a sleeping bag, toiletries, but also, more important, my bamboo flute and the painting utensils that would serve me during my vigil. I was not looking forward to spending the night in that densely crowded intensive care unit, which I had come to think of as an oversized incubator, containing patients struggling for their lives instead of babies. To stay in the warm, stagnant air and the eerie, hypnotic atmosphere for more than a couple of hours would be a real test. It would demand a heroic effort not just to fall over and faint.

When asked the day before, the nurses had had no objection to my moving in—in fact, they appeared to be rather relieved to turn one patient over to family care. Still, I made quite a stir among them when I arrived with my colorful pack, such as this ICU had most likely never seen before. I dropped everything next to my husband's bed and quickly pulled up a chair, eager to engage in conversation. Jürg squeezed out as many details as I could possibly give him of the happenings at home. Clearly, while his physical being was supported through infusions coming from the various suspended plastic bags through plastic lines into his arms, his psychic lifeline was attached to his family.

I cannot comprehend today that I did not have the courage to challenge Jürg's idea simply to be "gone" for a while and then return home, without allowing our children to visit him, their father, at the hospital. Did he really believe it would be less of a trauma for them to fantasize about the unknown than to witness reality? Moreover, how deeply in denial about his own emotional needs he must have been became evident in his thirst for news about his family.

Someone put a tray of food before the patient, a bowl of chicken broth, a small cup of yogurt, and a small cup of applesauce . . . not very nurturing, it seemed to me, and the calories provided could barely make up for the effort it took to imbibe the liquids. Jürg soon showed signs of exhaustion. I pulled out the flute and improvised until he drifted into sleep.

Looking at the clock was the only way to know what time of day it was in this windowless environment. The numbered circle that regulates our lives told me night was approaching. I started to prepare my quarters, rolling out the foam pad on the bare floor next to Jürg's bed, smoothing a cozy flannel sheet over it and arranging the red sleeping bag and the pillow on top. If it looked inviting, it was only because it brought back memories of past camping adventures. Once I was lying there, stretching out on my back and staring up at the shiny metal frame of the hospital bed, I fully realized the weird situation I found myself in. As the hours dragged on, with little sleep to make them pass more quickly, the night seemed interminable. My husband, on the other hand, slept like a baby, apparently reassured of my presence next to him. The idea of giving him relief was the only comfort I had besides, of course, my meditation.

Sometime during those long hours I sat up to paint, contemplate, and write. Gradually the insistent noise of the unit's machines softened and turned into background music, as if from far away. Space and time became indistinct. What emerged in my painting was an illustration of our situation, and yet to know myself as "the wise one" bending over the oracle filled me with awe, and I marveled at the healing effect it instilled. How could it be possible, I wondered, that I, tucked in next to a bed in the ICU of a university hospital in an American city, felt the necessity and indeed was able to establish a strong connection to the earth and to the ancient traditions of our ancestral past?

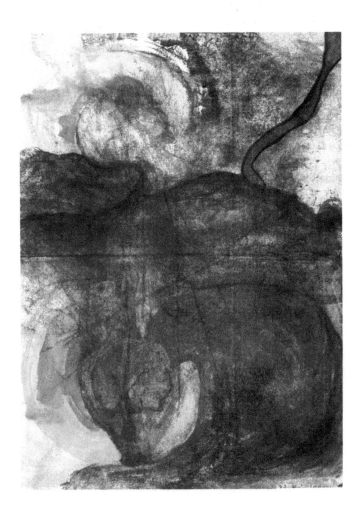

Heilenden Düften
aus tiefen Grüften
beugt sich der Weise entgegen in seiner Verborgenheit.
Sie steigen auf,
beleben den Schnauf
des Kranken, der an Schläuchen hängt,
und sein Schwanken wird leiser,
wo alles zur Heilung drängt.

Over healing vapors / arising from deep chasms /
the wise one is bending in her secret grove. /
They ascend, / enliven / the patient hanging on tubes /
and his trembling is calming / where healing is rushing in.

Thursday, 24 May

Jürg reported feeling refreshed after a good night's sleep and ready to make the move into a private room, scheduled for this day. It marked an important step on his journey back to health, as he was found stable enough to no longer need intensive care and supervision around the clock. He was looking forward to the transition, as much as one can in such a state of weakness and vulnerability. He particularly longed to reestablish a circadian rhythm, which was not afforded in the endless twilight of the ICU.

After breakfast, Jürg desired to sit up and make a painting himself. I arranged the bedside table, fetched a glass with water, and provided him with paper and the paint box I always carried around with me. For a long while he mixed the paints before he guided the brush onto the paper with an unsteady arm and a trembling hand, smearing as awkwardly as a three-year-old and with an equally engaged devotion. After he finished and put the brush down, he stared at his work intently and finally declared with a big sigh: "This is my face." It was a haunting image of devastation: a head without facial features, depicting the loss of sensory connection with the world and, symbolically, the temporary loss of a vision for the future. We did not voice such interpretations, however—there was no need. After the exercise Jürg was exhausted and fell back onto the pillow.

The impatient patient's desire to get on with life was in constant conflict with hospital protocol. During sleepless hours of the previous nights, Jürg apparently had developed a detailed plan of how he would get back on his feet, in the literal sense. Rather than wait for hospital personnel to assist him in their standardized ways, he intended to engage my help without the hospital's permission. I became a reluctant partner in crime, not wanting to cross my husband, yet neither wanting to stir up controversy in the hospital. Ultimately, though, my allegiance was to my husband.

The event of his first postoperative walk is forever marked in my memory or, more precisely, branded into the bones of my body. Much like the officer he had been in the Swiss army, Jürg explained to me with an air of author- ity exactly how the maneuver was going to happen. First he needed my help to sit up and scoot to the edge of the bed, which was a tiring exercise all by itself. Then I had to position myself on his right side, sitting on the edge as well, and sling his right arm around my neck. My left arm was to hold his lower back firmly, pulling his body close to mine. Our right hands were clasped together for more stability, while his left arm was swinging freely. As we were carefully arranging ourselves in this manner, I felt my heart cramp, suddenly aware of how weak my husband had become. He immediately picked up on my emotion and a hint of anger flushed his face. Neither of us said a word, however. Instead, I silently admonished myself to "empty my mind," the Zen attitude practiced for so many years, and to try to be fully present.

Thus we departed from his bed in slow motion, intertwined with each other like two strands of ivy. The exercise of mindfulness turned out to be extremely challenging for me, perhaps equal to the physical challenge for Jürg. Hanging, almost dangling, from my neck, attired in one of those flimsy, ridiculously short hospital gowns that barely cover the naked body under-neath—a shaky body that seemed to consist of nothing but skin and bones—and with his partly shaved head in a huge bandage, I could not help but think that he looked like a prisoner who had just escaped from a Nazi concentration camp. It terribly pained my heart. He could barely set one naked foot in front of the other, managing to do so only through his iron will and discipline. After a few short minutes we had to turn back abruptly, back to the safety of the hospital bed. The exercise instilled a strange mixture of hopeful satisfaction and despair: new steps had been taken, but much work lay ahead.

I was not present when the transition into the private room was accom-plished; supposedly it went smoothly. Meanwhile, I had the opportunity to greet my beloved in-laws at home. But when I came back in the evening for a visit in the private room, I found my husband changed, and not for the better. There he was, in a gloomy, deadly quiet room with naked walls in dark shades of purple and mauve, its only window facing the wall of an inner courtyard. It did not make for a cozy ambiance. The nurses' station seemed far away, and no one was around; coming from the womblike ICU, the unexpected loneli-ness must have been more shock than relief.

But I sensed that there was something deeper going on, something that made me feel uneasy. I had a hard time putting my finger on it, but I instinc-tively knew that I needed to be careful, even guarded about how I was relating to my husband. It was as if there had been a change in his personhood, initi-ated by the transition into the private room. Jürg's old, eminently respectable qualities had reemerged—his tremendous sense of responsibility and honor, his discipline and pride, the readiness to submit to hardship—but they were no longer accompanied by his formerly pronounced sense of humor and fun. Instead, they were paired with some more primitive and unpleasant emotions. Beneath the more superficial grumpiness and impatience, there seemed to be a profound rage emerging that felt like the distant rumbling thunder of an approaching storm.

When Jürg insisted that I should leave him alone and go home to be with the family, I left without argument and rather quickly, gladly even. Yet riding in the car, I suddenly felt overwhelmed by grief and by a host of depressing thoughts, doubts, feelings of hopelessness, and even a bad conscience. Did Jürg masochistically deprive himself? Had I been a coward? It dawned on me that getting through the operation was one thing, but going through the recovery would be quite another. I understood that the challenge for us, his family, was only just beginning, as Jürg was coming back into his body and reacting to the environment.

I chose light shades for my painting, quite in contrast to my brooding thoughts. Moreover, in a sudden impulse, I applied an untried crisscross folding pattern, perhaps in a rising premonition of approaching chaos. As it turned out, the cracks in the dried paint perfectly outlined the dove, and the suggestion of fire was there as well. With very little enhancement, I brought the disquieting image to completion, portraying what might be in store for me, for us: a trial by fire.

Die Taube muss durch's Feuer:
nichts ist geheuer.
Da ist rote Glut und gelbe Wut.
Des Teufel's Spitzel üben Nervenkitzel
an der armen Kreatur.
Wie, oh wie nur — Gott — lässt Du das zu,
und wann, oh wann, gibt es endlich Ruh?

The dove must go through the fire: / it is an uncanny event. /
There's glowing red and yellow dread / The devil's nasty helpers tickle the nervous
system / of the sorry creature. / How, just how — God — can this be true, /
and when, say when, will there be peace again?

Friday, 25 May

With great anticipation I brought Jürg's parents for a visit to the hospital in the morning, hoping they would boost his energy as they had mine. Alas, he was in a miserable state, complaining that his body had turned into a torture chamber, with an itching skin and tingling nerves "driving him insane," "making him crazy," as anticipated in my poem the night before. We wondered what was going on. Did the condition of his brain produce these symptoms, or was it the other way around? Jürg could barely contain his anger over some unpleasant confrontations he had had with the attending nurse during the night. There was no decency in his language when he shared what had happened. Apparently, the operation had stripped him of what social graces he once had possessed; he had none left and did not care in the least. Eventually, he relaxed, basked in the love and understanding that surrounded him, and was able to engage in a more civilized interaction. He took comfort in his mother's offer to stay overnight, as there was an extra bed in the room. I was secretly relieved as well.

On my own at night, however, I could not help but mix dark colors, grappling with the acutely felt sense of sinister foreboding. Sinking into my sad mood, I allowed ample time, folding the paper soaked with paint this way and that, slowly, carefully, in ritual gesture, only reluctantly opening it up again. A depressing scene revealed itself. The patterns in the dried paint looked frighteningly like barren tree trunks in a dark world. It became an image of Golgotha, the Christian symbol of suffering. When I gave faces to the two tree trunks in the center, it suddenly became very personally real.

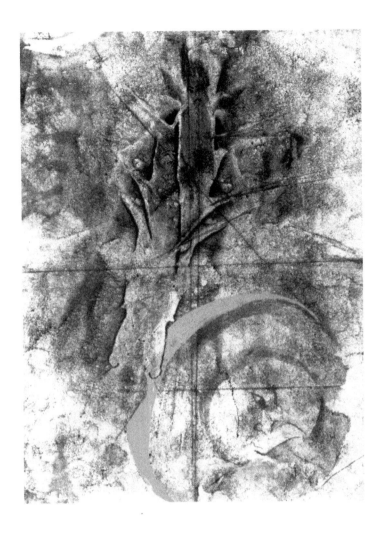

Es seufzen die Kreuze von Golgotha:
Wie lange, wie bange—
Längst vorbei und doch so nah.
Das Leiden nicht meiden:
heilig ist es immer da.
Der Mond denkt das Seine,
und ich weine.

The crosses at Golgotha are groaning and moaning: / How anxious, so long /
In the distant past, yet very real. / The suffering not to avoid: /
it is s a sacred presence. / The moon is dwelling in deep thoughts, /
And I am crying.

Saturday, 26 May

Things did not look good the next morning. When my father-in-law and I arrived at the hospital, we found two people in the gloomy hospital room who looked equally worn out and were exhibiting scarcely suppressed hostility, as if they had been at each other's throat. Eventually the story came out: how, in the middle of the night, Jürg had determined to take a warm bath to soothe his itching skin. He had asked his mother for help, but she had refused and recommended calling the nurse instead, rightly doubting that she was strong enough to assist him in and out of the tub. He, in turn, refused to involve the nurse, so she continued to object to the bath. The two, almost equally frail but equally endowed with a stubborn will, had quarreled with increasing anger, until the fight erupted into an archetypal mother-son struggle loud enough finally to attract a nurse's attention. My poor beloved mother-in-law! I thanked her in my heart for taking some of the heat, while wondering how we would be managing my husband at home, in just a few more days.

The daily walking exercise did not go well either, as my husband was trip-ping over his uncoordinated feet while venting his anger at his mother. I did my best to function in my combined roles of providing physical support and emotional buffering. My practice was simple: I acknowledged everything he said and did not object to anything he wanted to do, radiating unconditional love. In an odd blend of cowardice and wisdom, I knew that there was nothing else for me to do but to "hang in there," just as Jürg was hanging heavily from my neck during our walks. Most of the time I managed by not taking things personally, yet there were moments when I was acutely aware of my estrange-ment. Sometimes I even struggled with feelings of disgust that I could hardly admit to myself: my husband, the one I had known, loved, and respected, had turned into a strange being who harbored a wild beast inside! My only comfort was the felt sense that my daily excursions into imaginal space were instru-mental in transcending my personal vulnerability.

When I got around to my meditation, I crumpled the paper soaked with paint in my fist. It was a decidedly angry gesture, as if in compensation for my outward passivity. I held it firmly for a long while before I unfolded it again and smoothed it out. In midst of the chaotic network of crinkles in the black, intricate nebula, I saw a striking face emerge. In my ardent wish for Jürg to become his normal self again, I was intent on seeing him in this image, as . . . what was it? . . . of course, his hero—Lawrence of Arabia in Bedouin garb!

Ein neues Gesicht,
eine klare Sicht
entsteht im Puzzle der Welt.
Noch nicht auf die Beine gestellt,
noch fehlen Hand und Fuss—
es ist nur ein leiser Gruss:
ja,
ich bin wieder da!

A new face, / a new sight. / emerges from the world's puzzle. /
Not yet upright, / still lacking hands and feet, — / It's just a little wink: /
Yes, / I'm back again!

Sunday, 27 May

At last, homecoming day had arrived. We brought the patient in a wheelchair to the car, where we tucked him securely in the back. There he sat between his parents, wrapped in layers of cottons and woolens so as to pamper his vulnerable body and buffer his excitable nerves. The journey home was slow and subdued. Even my in-laws did not try to uphold their usually cheerful dispositions. We were wrapped up in thoughts and feelings, mine ranging from the relief of being released from the hospital to a cautiously celebratory mood in view of the family reunion to insecurity and a palpable apprehension of what was ahead.

The moment arrived when Jürg—son, husband, and father—stepped shakily over the threshold of our house, supported by a helpful arm on either side. The entrance was decorated with welcome banners and flowers. Our three children crowded around the door, watching the approaching procession with shy curiosity. In reaction to their obvious initial shock, they tried to be of service in any way imaginable.

The family den, which also served as Jürg's study, was going to be his bedroom for a while. It was a cozy room, with bookshelves lining the wall around the fireplace, his low Zen desk under the window, and a broad, low sofa filling out the opposite corner. Openings on three sides—into the living room, the dining room, and the porch—would allow him to be included in family life.

Something strange happened, however, although at first it was hardly perceptible. From the moment my husband was home, I became the focus of his negative attention, as had been the nurse and his own mother in the hospital. The idea that I should be the target of his poorly disguised rage came so unexpectedly that it caught me completely off guard. Was I not his loving wife? Had I not been the one to soothe and comfort him when he had been in distress? What was going on? He suddenly possessed a heightened awareness (was it by just sniffing the air?) of even the smallest imperfections or disorders in the household, which seemed to threaten his very existence. He turned against me, blaming me for everything that in his mind was wrong, calling me neglectful, egotistical, and other unsavory things.

I knew so well that I should not take it to heart—after all, he was a patient—but what he said, or yelled, hurt nevertheless and poisoned the atmosphere. Not that he was entirely "crazy"; he had enough of an ego to observe what was going on, but he could not suppress his negative emotions; he could not restrain that beast within him from acting out. The shadow, which I suppose he had disciplined so well and held under tight control, was breaking out of its civilized cage. Perhaps in compensation, Jürg anxiously and prematurely tried to reestablish his former modes of self-discipline and to think about and organize his future. For my part, I was wary and less willing to engage so soon in picking up the pursuit of his rigorous career. I was even questioning it, blaming, in my mind, the abusive medical system with its merciless surgical residency for my husband's illness.

We were at odds. Our psychic link was dangerously close to tearing apart, as we each felt abandoned by the other: Jürg in his desperate struggle to get back to health and on track as fast as possible and I in my innermost desire to simply huddle together with all my loved ones and express the pervasive but unacknowledged grief I felt. At least for once I needed us to cry, lament, wail, howl with the wolves together, without a thought for the future, until our hearts were emptied out. But, as before, I permitted myself only silent and secret tears, drawing further into myself. My husband, too weak to accomplish what he had in mind and sensing that his wife had slipped ever so subtly away (not from his care, to be sure, but from making future plans), gathered the confused family members to gang up against me, all the while suffering intensely and helplessly in his own state of miserable powerlessness. In the midst of our family, we both felt utterly alone. I longed to be comforted by my daily meditation.

On this night of homecoming, I found myself sitting alone in our bedroom again. As so many times before, the figures emerged from the paint as if on their own. I saw the fox and the doe come alive, reminiscent of Aesop's fables, with their symbolic qualities that readily lent themselves to an interpretation of aggression and submission, perpetrator and victim. I enhanced the dark shadow between them, which inadvertently took on the shape of a missile. Finally, a whitish lacuna within it evoked the dove, and I filled it in with thick white paste, in an upwelling of grim satisfaction. In my poem I captured the reflection of the image on our precarious situation.

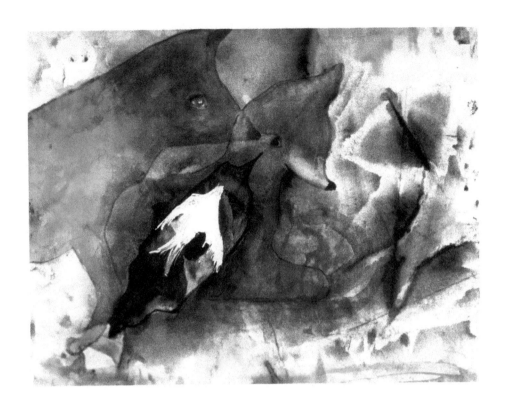

Diese ganze Zeit

ruhten Fuchs und Reh

zu zweit

und taten einander nicht weh.

Jetzt ballt sich Gewölke;

Gewitterregen prasseln nieder;

Geschosse fliegen durch die Luft.

Machen sie sich nun bereit,

die früheren feindlichen Brüder,

zum Streit?

Oder finden sie auf höherer Ebene sich wieder?

For all this time / fox and doe laid together, / and did not harm each other. /
But now a storm is brewing, / Heavy rain is pounding down; / missiles are flying
through the air. / Are they getting ready / those two inimical brothers / to fight? /
Or can they solve on a higher level their plight?

Monday, 28 May

Our elders—how devotedly they lived up to their mission to assist and support us! Noticing the rift opening between Jürg and me, they mobilized a seemingly endless supply of good humor and wisdom, filling the fissures with quotations from the ever-present grand father, Jung. They mended the fabric of our lives as best they could with stories from yesteryear and silly jokes, of which my father-in-law had an inexhaustible storehouse. In their spare time, Ignaz painted meaningful Egyptian hieroglyphs on the tiles around the fireplace, which Sabi then crowned with a Latin saying that many days later would suddenly come alive with meaning in a painting: *Res sacra miser* ("Illness is a sacred matter").

While watching them walking down the street together toward the supermarket, with the wire shopping cart on two wheels trailing behind them, I was reminded of the mythic figures Philemon and Baucis. These two old ones knew how to host divine spirits and how to invite their presence into daily life with its humble chores. They did not mind shopping daily for fresh strawberries, because that was all Jürg wanted to eat: strawberries with cornflakes and milk, and not only for taste, but also for the colors' symbolism. The red and white reminded him of the Swiss flag, he told us, and therefore of his native roots.

Our children, stunned witnesses of what they saw happening, adapted as best they could. The girls, intimidated by the unpredictable currents of emotions and irrational moods, behaved like two little mice, always on the lookout for the closest hole they could hide in. Our son, the oldest, on the other hand, rose to the challenge of becoming a pillar of strength and support practically overnight, for which his father was ostensibly grateful.

Tuesday, 29 May

This date marked our engagement anniversary, much to our embarrassment, for we were not in a disposition to celebrate. The general mood in the house remained subdued and sullen. Jürg held a secretive meeting with his parents in the study, to which I had not been invited. Bitterness dwelled in my heart while I was going absentmindedly about my household chores, feeling treated like Cinderella. Later in the day, my mother-in-law whispered a warning into my ear. Jürg had invited them to discuss his medications "exclusively among medical peers." In spite of the counsel of his doctors and his father's cautiously voiced concerns, he had made a case to begin weaning himself prematurely from what I believe were prescribed antipsychotic medications, convinced that he could master his mind and his emotions just as he had before the operation. As he had done in the hospital, the patient acted as his own physician, but this time it would not turn out to be to anyone's benefit.

I surrendered to the inevitable and unknown, resolving to simply do what needed to be done. I welcomed the image of that night's meditation as a reflection of the situation. I captured its meaning mostly in projection: "he," my hero, deeply hidden in the belly of the cancer—a symbol that took on ominous multiple meanings in its relation with the Great Mother, the unconscious, and the illness—but then there also was a sense of a mystery that concerned me, something in the depth of my psyche.

A few uneventful days passed, just trying to get on with life, while carefully watching the patient's moods and needs. All the while, the young ones were encouraged to pursue their regular activities. Our older daughter's journal is a moving testimony of how they tried to cope with their split world. On June 3, about to graduate from junior high school, she started the first of an ongoing series of journals. This was her first entry, addressing a fictitious "other":

> Did I tell you about my dad? He had a brain tumor. He's been operated by the best doctor and then we stold him home so he could recover faster. He can't walk right yet, or see strait, or . . . I could go on forever, but it would get too sad and all we have to do is have patience. This is the hardest thing for my dad—he has absolutely zero patience. So he has a lot of spaz-attacks, and the victim is my poor mom (nurse 24 hours a day, no break).

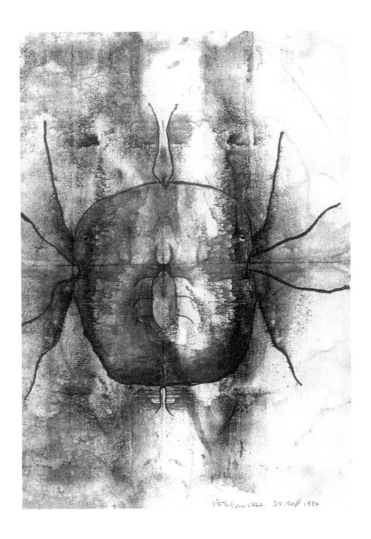

Im Krebs haust er,

tief unten im Meer;

verschluckt oder dort gewachsen?

Hirschkäfer zeigt nicht sein prächtig Geweih,

und niemand weiss dass dem so sei:

In der dunklen Schale liegt das Glück vesteckt—

keiner sagt, er hab's geweckt . . .

He lives in the crab, / in the ocean's bottomless depths; / swallowed or grown there? /
The stag beetle doesn't display its gorgeous antlers / and nobody knows about it: /
In the dark shell luck lies hidden — / no one says to have awakened it . . .

Thursday, 31 May

The last morning in May arose in quiet beauty, lingering in the cool, aromatic air before gathering strength to lift its wings. Waking up refreshed from sleep before the house stirred always put me into a celebratory mood. How long had it been since I had had the luxury of doing a morning meditation? As I prepared my painting materials I wondered where it came from, this unexpected flurry of joy. Was it a heightened vibration in the lovely spring air that moved my psyche, or was it a movement in my psyche that apprehended the world in its beauty?

Whatever it was, the painting with its subtle folds brought about the surprising "birth" of the imaginary stag beetle in its full size and magnificence. While enhancing its circumference in black, and then its coat in deep blue and gold, I felt overwhelmed with gratitude—now my joy was embodied.

I had the distinct impression that something had been born within me, too, and along with it there arose the desire, or the courage rather, to share my paintings with the family. Admittedly, in a secret chamber of my heart there was a hint of hope that my work would redeem my being so ill considered, so basically at fault and inadequate. These pictures were the language of soul, and my family was receptive to that language and understood it well.

My announcement that I had something for show-and-tell was received with a mixture of benevolence and skepticism. I did not let it get to me, however, for this was the last weekend before Jürg's parents would leave us again, and thus my last opportunity to share my artwork with them as well. After breakfast, we assembled in the den that had become Jürg's dwelling place. He was sitting cross-legged on the sofa wearing the Japanese kimono a Zen friend had given him, and his presence produced little butterflies in my stomach and a trembling in my heart. But my strong resolve overcame any hesitation.

Once everyone had found a comfortable spot and settled, I took a deep breath and started. After a brief introduction of how I came to paint the way I did and what it meant to me, I pulled up the first painting. After a pause, I read the poem. With neither hurry nor delay I moved on to the next one, then the next, and so on, briefly recalling salient events of each day as I had recorded them. The mood in the room was changing. The members in our family had become quiet, almost transfixed; the air regained the transparency and vibrancy of early morning. I had a felt sense of our souls mingling and dancing with each other.

The paintings had transformed the most painful experience in my life into healing images and poetry. Now I witnessed with amazement the effect they had on my family. From the corner of my eye, I saw that my husband had a smile on his face, and I could feel his armor melt away. When I came to the last of my paintings I ended with a deep sigh: "Well, this is it." The silence endured for a while, heavy and peaceful, until the young ones stirred. The grandparents murmured words of appreciation; my father-in-law, as always, spontaneously offered his commentary. Jürg was apologetic and humbly expressed how he had treated me unjustly. His words dripped like balm onto a festering wound.

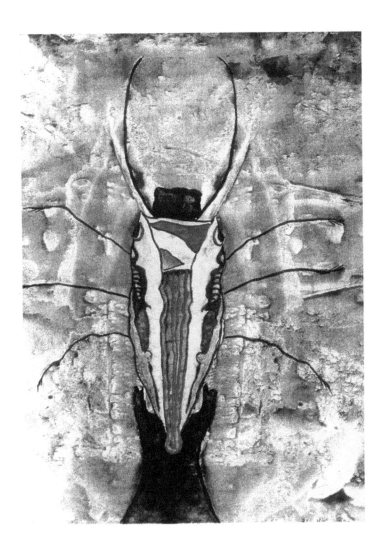

Er hat's vollbracht,
über Nacht.
Hat die Schale zerbrochen
und ist ausgekrochen—
Ich muss ihm Nahrung geben.
Gott, hilf Du ihm zum Leben!

He did it, / over night. / He broke the shell / and crawled into the light— /
I must provide the food for him. / God, you will help him live!

Tuesday, 5 June

Alas, the reconciliatory mood that had descended like a blessing over the inhabitants of our house would not last. Within a few days it faded. Was it the effect of Jürg weaning himself off the psychotropic medications that stirred up emotions? Or was it the approaching end of his parents' visit that raised unacknowledged anxiety? To the degree that I relented and lost my newly acquired self, Jürg felt the necessity to act as the responsible head of household. He became obsessed with keeping everything and everybody under control, while being himself quite out of control. The free space that my paintings had opened in our hearts was closing up again; there was no room for the souls to dance, and apparently no room in Jürg's mind to ponder the meaning of his illness or to wonder about the future. Questioning whether he really would be up to joining the transplant team in Sacramento, rather than staying for a while longer in Chicago, let alone moving back to Switzerland, would excite his irascibility. He had set his mind on Sacramento because anything else apparently signified defeat.

Jürg had me find the file in his desk that contained a bundle of forms related to his new position and demanded that I fill them out. Perhaps he needed tangible proof of his decision. What prompted me at that moment to argue instead of complying, to attempt to convince him that filling out these forms was premature and unnecessary, I do not know. Was it an irrational spark of rebellion against his outrageous domination? Was it the barely awakened and still awkward voice of my own emerging authority? Or simply a desperate last attempt to resist the course of events? To my own disbelief, I refused to acquiesce. As if talking to a normal person, I set out to discuss why these forms could wait until after we had actually found a new domicile and moved, which was objectively true and reasonable enough. The odd glimmer in Jürg's eyes did not deter me. Suddenly, he tried to stand up on the mattress of the sofa bed, awkwardly balancing his shaky and trembling body in a mounting rage. He grabbed my arm with one hand and then, quite unexpectedly, started to beat me with the other, while yelling wild accusations. He could not really hurt me physically, for he was too weak to do any sort of harm—it was my spirit he was beating up. The incident stirred up great emotions. His parents came running to hold him back and to free me from the assault. While they tried to calm him down, I ran out into the yard, overcome with crying and shaking.

The rest of the day is still a blur in my mind. Jürg and I never talked about the incident again. In the process of writing and remembering, however, I asked my adult children about it. This time, my son had a vivid memory. He recalled how he found me in the backyard, a sorry bundle of tears, when he came home from school. "I wanted to run in and kill my dad," he said, "but then I found him in shambles, and his pitiful state immediately disarmed me. I did my best to comfort him and could not understand how you could have had the nerve to provoke him so—an ill man—and not simply pay attention to what you knew would help him to recover!" Of course I agreed in hindsight, while a sense of shame rose within me, overshadowing righteousness and self-pity.

My older daughter, who at the time had always turned to her diaries, was now willing to "dig them up," although she had not looked at them for many years. We delved into them as into another world, another lifetime, and found what we were looking for: as expected, she had taken refuge in there during the crisis, scared and lonely, apparently unable to turn to anyone for help. Here is her entry for this day:

> Oh God! Help my mom not give up. Help her fight!! Today my dad was the most aggressive I've ever seen him. He bossed my mom around like a slave. She had to fill out forms for him and then he wanted to see them (this is what I heard when I came home from softball—we won 20 to 4). Then I walked in the door and see a pillow fly through the air—my dad screaming at the top of his lungs "get out" or something, and my mom bawling. Mom won't take any comfort from me, I knew that, so I stayed away 'til she went to her room.

It moved me deeply, especially her statement that I would not take any comfort from her. Another wave of shame welled up, belatedly—this one over our mother-daughter relationship that had been so deficient. I don't remember my daughter coming to my room in the evening, nor do I have a recollection of what had transpired before. I believe that the situation seemed too hopeless, in the moment, to be repaired, and everyone just withdrew into his or her own quarters.

There I found myself on my carpet, crushed by the events, smearing black paint over a golden ground to reflect our state of profound despair that had overshadowed—nay, swallowed—the golden moment of a few days ago. In slow motion, I folded the paper crosswise, then rubbed it mechanically with my fist, quite certain that nothing would come of this one, and I wouldn't care. Similar to the night of my first painting, I stared into the void. This time, though, it was the abyss of my own wretchedness. When I finally opened the folded paper again, I was momentarily baffled: the blackness was not dead but very much alive! What stood out immediately was the small Buddha figure sitting cross-legged, adorned with a fanlike headdress rising from a narrow black band. But then, while contemplating the darkness, I came to recognize the oval outline of a face and traced the features in it with increasing awe: the hollow of a downcast eye, the sharp ridge of the nose, a gently smiling mouth . . . it was Buddha's face. As it were, the small Buddha or monk figure came to sit exactly at the location of the third eye.

Sitting in the deep silence of the night, I was stunned and humbled. I distinctly felt that I had just received a gift from the gods, as unexpected as it was undeserved. The gift was complete; there was no need to contribute anything to the painting by my own effort. I intuitively understood the image as a message about acceptance of the dark side of human nature, the shadowy side of who we were, and of redemption. But I shied from crafting such notions into a poem. What came to mind, instead, were the Latin words written onto the mantle of the fireplace: *Res sacra miser*.

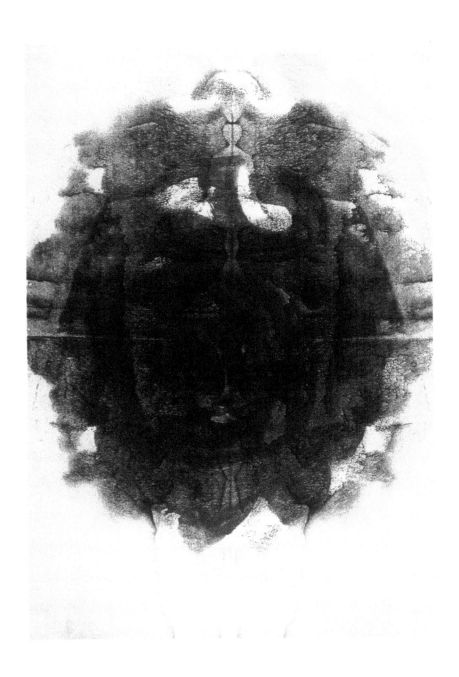

Res sacra miser.

Illness is a sacred matter.

Tuesday, 19 June

During the transitional period between the departure of Jürg's parents and the arrival of his older sister as further support, he and I were carefully trying to mend the rift between us. But we were both feeling too sobered and down-cast to kindle the spark of love and trust that we were yearning for so badly. There is no artwork from that period, probably because the responsibilities for my husband's care, the children, and the household were resting on my shoulders; besides, most of Jürg's attention was focused on me, leaving me neither the physical nor the psychic space for a retreat.

Jürg's sister, Roswith, brought a fresh wind into our house. With her expert knowledge in body awareness and relaxation exercises, rhythmics, and music, she exerted an immensely positive influence on our family. Jürg turned into a peaceful and obedient lamb in her presence; his mental status and his physical condition improved markedly. One day, he felt confident and strong enough to risk climbing the stairs to the second floor, if only for the purpose of exercise. Roswith, teaching him how to use his muscles correctly, moved alongside step by step while the rest of the family cheered him on and cel-ebrated his achievement once he made it to the top. This, it turned out, was how a triumphant husband moved back into the marital bedroom. I succinctly remember that moment: how I genuinely wanted to share in the joy and welcome him back into our room, as it marked such an important step in the progress of Jürg's recovery. Yet, I found myself suppressing an embarrassing impulse to defend my privacy in this space that had become so essential to my well-being. Of course, I had no choice but to let things happen and make a genuine effort at accommodation.

The variety of creative activities guided by Roswith absorbed many ill feel-ings and kept strengthening our bonds. She had us carve our own bamboo flutes, each a little piece of art, compose melodies, and use song and move-ment. She broke new ground for us and tilled the soil so that it could nurture new growth and bear fruit; she soothed and mended the wings of our crushed spirits until our souls dared to move again and dance. She had endless patience, deeply grounded in her practices.

The soil of my psyche had been well fertilized through my own imaginal activity, to which the series of paintings was a living testimony. I had under-gone a transformation and was open to allowing a new self to come to the fore, one grounded in a femininity that was more at ease and self-accepting. When, after many days, I was able to steal a moment for a painting, I was in a positive frame of mind and chose accordingly vivid colors. Even as I put the finishing touches to the image, I fell in love with the vibrantly healthy animals

and marveled over the glowing red globe. The sense of personal empower-
ment, experienced at the stag beetle's birth, had returned. But although I was
aware that the emerging energy was more grounded at this point, I implored
myself, in the poem, to contain the exuberance, afraid that it might inadvertently turn into its opposite, as before.

Paradoxically, with this painting the inner resistance to my husband's
unequivocal resolve to move to Sacramento *as soon as possible* lessened; I
found both my own vision and the courage to do what needed to be done.
Jürg, in turn, welcomed my awakened authority and leadership abilities and
increasingly made demands upon them.

Die Glut soll nicht brennen lichterloh,

nur eine kleine Kerze speisen — denn sowieso

muss das Huhn erst brüten, brüten,

um ein Unglück zu verhüten.

Dann ist das Wotanross bereit

und auf geht's wie der Wind, zu zweit!

The glow shall not turn to blasting fire, / just feed a little candle — because /
the hen first has to brood and brood / to avert misfortune. /
Then Wotan-horse will be prepared / to carry us off, fast as the wind!

Tuesday, 26 June

There was yet another prolonged interval before this last painting came into being. I had returned from a trip to Sacramento, where, in the company of my father, I had found a new home for our family. It was within walking distance of the hospital, where the transplant team was awaiting Jürg's full recovery and arrival.

A huge task was ahead of me. I was to sell our beloved home in Chicago "by owner," pack up its contents, and prepare the family to move, all the while caring for my physically and emotionally challenged partner. The period of "brooding and breeding" was over; the moment to act had arrived.

This last painting, which naturally seemed to bring the series to an end, was a vivid reflection of my new self as a woman happily in her power in a way I had never before known or thought possible for myself.

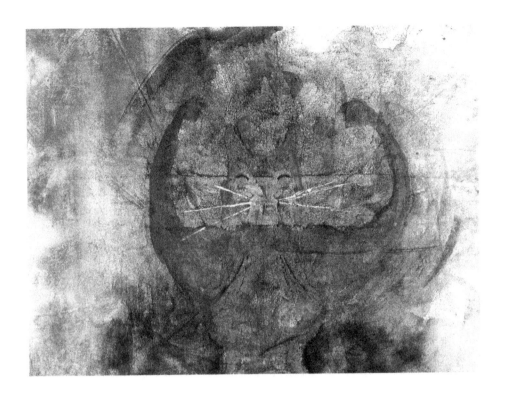

Katze
mit der lustigen Fratze
erhebt ihre Tatze:
"schau, ich bin ja Frau!
             Miauuuuhh . . . "

Cat / with a funny hat / is raising her paws: / "Look, I am woman!" / Meaowhhh . . . . "

Commentary

Painting 1

Here, then, is the painting that initiated the series. Like initial dreams that people bring into analysis, this picture set the stage for what wanted to come.

The image shows a simple symmetry with a vertical central axis, created by the one fold through the middle. The horizontal axis was introduced by painting the line that separates the sky from the sea. A heavy black arch looms over the water, carving out a space infused with golden light and with a dramatic red globe in its center. Surprisingly, many of the decorative lines on the globe, which I had introduced at whim, look similar to the symbols for the metals used by the alchemists (see Elkins 2000). From the top of the red globe sprout two flowering twigs, branching out symmetrically on either side. A long arrow is drawn along the central axis, pointing down toward the lower margin. There, seemingly below the ocean, the golden light reappears.

This first painting is a bit awkward and aesthetically less satisfying than the ones that followed. It does not yet exhibit the fine-tuned awareness of how psyche wants to reveal itself in the patterns of dried paint that would guide me for the rest of the series. There is a certain heavy-handedness in its treatment, as I had allowed myself to willfully assert an optimistic outlook by introducing a foreign element nowhere suggested in the textures of the dried paint: the two flowering twigs. On the other hand, I had overlooked a subtle shape visible in the dried paint that was waiting to be discovered and elaborated, its symbolism equally suggestive and promising to what I had added out of ego's fancy.

The poem invokes "one who has sunken deep" (*Tiefversunkener*). In retrospect, the address seems ambiguous: I obviously had my husband Jürg in mind—he who would literally sink deep into unconsciousness during the operation, induced by the anesthesia. But in German, the word also means "one who is in deep contemplation or meditation," which, then, would refer to myself.[7] The same ambiguity pertains to the notion of "drinking the bloody cup." Did I have Jürg in mind, submitting as a patient to the "bloody surgery," to the pain and suffering in the aftermath, or had I encouraged myself with this metaphor, to face the trial, struggling with a sinking feeling and a foreboding of dark and difficult times to come? In both instances, it is probably not either/ or, but both/and.

I interpreted the black arch as a black rainbow sinking into the ocean. It is a strange image, for generally the sight of a rainbow, arched between earth and sky in its transparently colored beauty, is uplifting and instills a sense of promise. Since ancient times, research tells me, rainbows have been revered as intermediaries and pathways between heaven and earth, "bridges used by gods and heroes when they travel between this Earth and the Otherworld" (Chevalier and Gheerbrant 1969, p. 783). The rainbow bridge was even considered the *axis mundi*, or ladder of heaven, over which deities, spirits, and mortals passed back and forth easily. In the earliest known cultures, however, the softly shimmering rainbow is said to have belonged to the goddess. Its seven colors represented the veils of Maya in Hinduism and of Salome in the Bible; in Egyptian mythology, they were the seven stoles of Isis; in Sumer, they were the garments or the necklace of the goddess Ishtar. However, I have also come across the notion of a darker aspect of the rainbow, which is less well known: in some ancient or indigenous traditions, the rainbow conjured up images of the mythic "perilous sky-serpent" (ibid., p. 785), which was seen as an omen of sickness and death or a prologue to disturbances of universal harmony (a universal catastrophe). By calling the arch in the painting a black rainbow, I had unwittingly drawn on the sinister aspect of the archetypal symbol.

Moreover, the rainbow in my painting is not only black, it is also sinking into the ocean, and one has to surmise that it will pull the red globe underwater along with it. Symbolically, such a red round object would be associated with the sun as the center of our planetary system and with the heart as the center of the human body; psychologically, it may represent the core of one's personality—in Jungian terms, the Self.[8] But given the real life crisis situation, the red globe in my poem had taken on a sinister connotation as well, imagined dramatically as a "bloody cup" that must be imbibed. Besides the associations touched on above (the cup as one's fate that must be accepted), the most mysterious tales woven around the image of the bloody cup involve the archetypal symbolism of the Holy Grail. In Christian mythology, this is the chalice used by Christ at the last supper and the cup in which the blood of the crucified was collected (the Eucharist, believed to hold the real blood of Christ during the Catholic Mass). Astoundingly, when traced farther back to ancient, prepatriarchal symbolism, the origin of the grail is found in the divine feminine mysteries. Walker writes: "Like the Celts' holy Cauldron of Regeneration, which it resembled, the blood-filled vessel was a womb symbol, meaning rebirth in the Oriental or Gnostic sense of reincarnation" (1983, p. 352). Neumann, too, emphasizes the importance of the vessel as a feminine symbol: "The vessel lies at the core of the elementary character of the Feminine. At all stages of the primordial mysteries it is the central symbol of their realization" (1955, p. 282). These were mysteries of preservation, formation, nourishment, or transformation. Thus, the vessel is the container within which matter is transformed—cooked or allowed to ferment, made into medicine, poison, or intoxicant. Neumann asserts that "this transformation, which is viewed as magical, can only be effected by the woman, because she herself, in her body that corresponds to the Great Goddess, is the caldron of incarnation, birth, and rebirth" (ibid., p. 287–288). The measures women traditionally used in preparation for magic and manticism included isolation, hunger, the infliction of pain, the consumption of intoxicants, the drinking of blood, or poisoning with herbal or vegetable substances.[9] On the level of the deep unconscious psyche, then, the bloody cup is aligned with ancient female wisdom traditions, of which I had no conscious awareness at the time of painting.

Last we come to the subtle form I had overlooked at the time. It is found at the narrowest spot of the hourglass shape in the water underneath the red globe. There it is by its own accord: the effigy of a horned animal, perfectly represented in the dried paint. The head is framed by a kind of square collar around its neck, and the intelligent eyes are looking directly at us. Oddly, I hadn't noticed it in spite of the black and red arrow's tip pointing exactly down to it; at the time, I didn't have the awareness to attach any special meaning to it. Now I have the opportunity to pay homage to this image, which, in symbolic significance, assumes an equally important place in ancient and contemporary mythological imaginings as that of the goddess: the Horned God, also known as the Lord of Animals or the Wild Man. He will return in various images throughout the series, until such moment when I *would* recognize him (if only by its highly numinous effect) in painting 14.

For my research, I have taken advantage of Robert Bly's exploration of the archetype. Tracing the history of the Wild Man since his first appearance, Bly suggests that the imaginative leap leading to the vision of the Lord of Animals (part human, part god, part animal) was a great religious event, parallel to but distinct from the imagining of "a compassionate, nourishing, abundant, ruthless being, a Birth Mother and Grave Mother" (1990, p. 238)—the one whom Marija Gimbutas calls with certainty "the Great Goddess." Bly describes the Horned God as "the god of depth, wounds, and sacrifice," quoting Mircea Eliade, who said that he regards the Master of the Hunt as "the most divine figure in all prehistory" and therefore "the prototype of all subsequent gods," in particular of the Greek Dionysus who came later (ibid., p. 240). The earliest known historic testimonies reside in the neighboring sanctuaries from the Paleolithic, some 20,000 to 25,000 years ago, in the south of France, known as the caves of Lascaux and Trois Frères, respectively. Throughout the Celtic societies in Europe, the Lord of Animals was known as Cernunnos (Cornely or Cornelius), the Horned One. The finest, and perhaps best known, image is preserved on a cauldron found in Jutland, the Gundestrup cauldron. Cernunnos is depicted sitting in a yogalike posture surrounded by animals, holding a serpent in his left hand and a torque in his right. He has a human face with a meditative expression, and he is wearing a sort of cap with antlers attached. Patricia Damery offers a delightful description of the Puck Fair in Ireland, suspecting that its roots lie in the pagan festival of Lughnasadh, a sacred Celtic fertility celebration at the beginning of harvest. Yet speculations point to an even earlier, pre-Celtic origin of the myth, which (not a surprise) revolved around the goddess and her consort: the Horned God. From a Jungian perspective, Damery suggests, the Horned God embodies "an animus function or masculine attitude that is also related to the body, that touches the psychoid levels of the psyche" (2004, p. 24). If taken seriously as an inner dynamic to be reckoned with, the Horned God can be "an important consultant, because he mediates—not by conquering, but by working closely with these life forces that include energies we repress: sexuality, aggression, violence, hatred, rage" (ibid., p. 20–21). By addressing the shadowy personal and cultural complexes, we build an ego structure that can hold the original animal vitality of the Horned God. He then becomes the guardian of our psyche's integrity. Moreover, the way Sherry Salman puts it in her essay on the Horned God, he also seems to share aspects with the alchemical Mercurius:

> The Horned God represents the guardian, healer, and shape shifter who mediates the world of the objective psyche. He is the elusive, transformative substance of the psyche itself—the adversary (Devil or Antichrist) *and* the savior who, with one hand, protects the Mysteries from destructive influences and, with the other, protects the human psyche from contact with what it cannot bear. Encountering him involves a confrontation with the objective psyche and our own limitations, one of the essential tasks of psychotherapy. (1986, p. 7)

For the Celtic priests, the Druids, Cernunnos was the mediator between ordinary reality and the otherworld. In Damery's interpretation, accessing the energy of the Horned God and the goddess requires an altered, or nonordinary, state of consciousness. I would think that anybody practicing a form of meditation or active imagination is very familiar with such a state of mind. In summary, then, the downward arrow, pointing exactly to the third eye of the horned animal, energized the potential of the powerfully dynamic animus lingering in the darker recesses of my psyche.

McNiff (1992), commenting on his own active imaginations through the medium of painting, notes how an image evokes different feelings, reactions, and interpretations at different times. Even more so, an as yet undifferentiated inkblot (or, in my case, paint blot) brings up imaginal associations fitting one's psychic disposition and situational reality at any given time. Whereas, at the time of crisis, I saw a black rainbow sinking into the ocean, I now behold the picture in its entire gestalt and see the stylized head of a woman with dense black hair. Most of her face is covered by the red globe, and the lower part is submerged under the agitated waters. In that case, the image of the horned animal comes to sit exactly in the woman's throat. Thus, quite fittingly in light of my passion for singing, the Dionysian element is located in its appropriate place: the vocal cords.

Where alchemy is concerned, the dissolution of aggregates in water is often considered the initial operation of the opus, known as *solutio*. Water was a metaphor for the womb, and the return of differentiated matter to its original undifferentiated state, the *prima materia*, represented a return to the womb for rebirth "and emerging from the water is a repetition of the act of creation in which form it was first expressed" (Mircea Eliade, quoted in Edinger 1985, p. 58). The imagery of my first painting and poem unmistakably displays the theme of *solutio*: the black arc, along with the red disc, sinking into the ocean. Edinger's comment that "major life transitions are commonly *solutio* experiences" (ibid., p. 47) is all too fitting: indeed, Jürg and Mar (as I was called at the time), husband and wife, were fated to undergo dissolution of old external and internal structures, just like Sol and Luna or Rex and Regina in the old alchemical texts.

Solutio symbolism is known to contain many aspects of the Dionysian principle, and thus we have come back around to the Horned God. In my painting, his effigy is immersed in water, true to Otto's statement: "[Dionysus] has his place of refuge and home in the watery depths" (quoted in Edinger 1985, p. 60). But Dionysian rites also included the dismemberment of a sacrificial victim, a fate that Christ embodied later in history. The alchemists were well aware of the inherent danger in *solutio*, which is why they commonly associated it with the *nigredo* ("blackening") and frequently gave negative imagery to the experience. In association with Dionysus, then, *solutio* might turn into *mortificatio* (literally "killing"), referring to the experience of death, fragmentation, and dismemberment. As the alchemists realized, "that which is being dissolved will experience the *solutio* as an annihilation of itself" (Edinger 1985, p. 52). On a literal level, a major modern-day operation might well be regarded as the equivalent of such an experience. In fact, it is uncanny how our situation was paralleled by the alchemist's characterization of the beginning of the opus as "a time of bloodshed and lamentation" (Abraham 1998, p. 135). The alchemist Fabricius, commenting on the opening emblem of Trismosin's *Splendor Solis*, says, "Its season of spring is a season of sacrifice, its river a life stream of blood" (ibid.). It cast a shadow over the alchemist, and he or she suffered from despair and melancholia. I am stunned by how vividly my initial painting, together with the poem, portrays these potent alchemical themes.

Speaking about alchemy during an interview, Jung stated, "the alchemical opus is dangerous. Right at the beginning you meet the 'dragon,' the chthonic spirit, the 'devil' or, as the alchemists called it, the 'blackness,' the *nigredo*, and this encounter produces suffering" (quoted in Edinger 1985, p. 147). Indeed, we shall meet the devil right away.

Painting 2

It looks as if the red globe, the "bloody cup," had just exploded. The bursting reds and oranges portray the intense emotionality I felt on that morning of my husband's operation. Rather than helplessness, denial, and grief, there was anger and rage arising against the tumor, and through the choice of colors I was in touch with these emotions and gave them expression.

The particular handling of paper and paint had established itself as my method of experimentation. Again, the central fold is used as a vertical division to create a left-right symmetry. As a painter, I had come into my element very quickly. We can see here how the finishing touches only enhance what is already present in the paint; they are used sparingly and applied more carefully than in the first painting.

The devil is seemingly falling from the sky—"out of the blue"—with a certain heaviness, like a meteorite or a piece of winged lead. He looks primitive and theriomorphic, with hoofs not only on his feet but on his hands as well.

These and the small horns and pointed ears, along with the wily, mischievous smile, betray who he is. The four-pointed wings in a U shape and the black feather collar add to his mythical appearance. He has come between the couple and burst it asunder. The explosions are located at the level of the heart, indicating that it is a highly emotional experience. Only a thin thread is still connecting the two people. The man to the left and the woman to the right are in shock, watching each other or the monster in stunned silence.

Already with this second painting, I had established a process I learned to trust and actively engage in, increasingly able to let go of wishful ego-thinking and be open to look, see, and accept "the soul's ministrations." In daring to expose myself to the full impact of the living and healing symbols revealed in the dried paint (my alembic), I would gain strength, in turn, to accept life as it presented itself. "Seeing the devil," though, was a truly startling experi- ence. And acknowledging his presence by unflinchingly painting his features was a bit like holding my own feet to the fire, but there had been no doubt in my mind that this devil was the personification of my husband's tumor. What had been, at least in part, a complex of my own I could recognize only in projection. The tumor's masculine gender in the German language had made the association easy. Notably, the poem is the only one of the whole series composed in English: the devilish tumor was an embodied evil, which, in my mind, could have grown only in the United States, never in my idealized homeland, and thus he had to be addressed in English. In a secret corner of my mind, I had harbored bitter feelings against a culture where the medical establishment put such exigent demands on surgical residents. Perhaps even more suppressed, however, was a lingering resentment against Jürg himself, whose career had brought the family into that culture and held it in such a tight grip of prolonged hardship. Throughout the years since the emigration, this remained a shadowy complex, never properly given voice—not even with all the singing I did.

Incidentally, associations between tumor, devil, and complex are found in Jung's writings. In "A Review of the Complex Theory," he gives a dramatic description of the destructive side of complexes, adding, "one could best compare them with infections or with *malign tumours*, both of which arise without the least assistance from the conscious mind" (1948a, par. 209, emphasis added). And in the third Tavistock Lecture, Jung talks about being "hampered by those little devils, the complexes" (1935, par. 151). With my disregard for what the devil could have meant for my own being, the psycho- logical hellfire we encountered during the difficult period of recovery perhaps burned hotter between us, the couple. At any rate, the stuff would promptly emerge from the unconscious later, and I found myself forced to address it, which I did through my meditative process.

The devil, or Satan, as an archetypal figure, has a long history. Jung writes about his development:

> The figure of Satan, too, has undergone a curious development, from his first undistinguished appearance in the Old Testament texts to his heyday in Christianity. He achieved notoriety as the personification of the adversary or principle of evil, though by no means for the first time, as we meet him centuries earlier in the ancient Egyptian Set and the Persian Ahriman. Persian influences have been conjectured as mainly responsible for the Christian devil. (1952a, par. 470)

Walker refers to the Christian devil as a "composite of ancient deities in a single Protean form" (1983, p. 226). The goat horns and hoofs are reminiscent of the satyrs, Pan, and Dionysus; he has a trident like Neptune, Hades, or Shiva; the reptilian form is that of Leviathan or Python; the fiery form comes from Agni or Helios; the female breasts he sometimes displays are borrowed from Ishtar/Astarte, and the quadruple wings from the Babylonian cherubim. The devil in my painting exhibits many of the mentioned attributes, which is remarkable, as I simply had followed the patterns in the paint and used my imagination. Interestingly, Walker also notes that, etymologically,

> the words "devil" and "divinity" grew from the same root, the Indo-European *devi* (Goddess) or *deva* (God), which became *daeva* (devil) in Persian. Old English *divell* (devil) can be traced to the Roman derivative *divus, divi*: gods. (Ibid., p. 225)

Thus, Walker concludes, since ancient times, gods and devils were often confused with one another: "Divine and devilish were relative terms, as was the primary sense of Hebrew 'beneficial' and 'hurtful'" (ibid.). In Jung's view, it was Milton, in *Paradise Lost*, who "exalted [the devil] to a cosmic figure of first rank" and "apostrophize[d] him as the true *principium individuationis*" (1952a, par. 470). He gave, Jung writes, poetic substance to a concept that the alchemists had anticipated some time before.

In alchemy, the devil in Milton's sense is embodied by the spirit Mercurius, "a redeeming psychopomp, an evasive trickster, and God's reflection in physical nature" (Jung, 1948b, par. 284). As the agent of all transmutation, the alpha and omega of the alchemical opus, Jung considers him "verily the principle of individuation":

Mercurius is not only the counterpart of Christ in so far as he is the 'son' [*filius*]; he is also the counterpart of the Trinity as a whole in so far as he is conceived to be a chthonic triad. According to this view he would be equal to one half of the Christian Godhead. He is indeed the dark chthonic half, but he is not simply evil as such, for he is called "good *and* evil," or a "system of the higher powers in the lower." He calls to mind that double figure which seems to stand behind both Christ and the devil—that enigmatic Lucifer whose attributes are shared by both. (Ibid., par. 271)

Mercurius's affinity with the devil is most pronounced at the very beginning of the alchemical opus, when he rises as the chthonic spirit from the dark earth, in association with the *nigredo* and the *mortificatio*. Mortification does not have a chemical equivalent; it has to do, Edinger writes, with "the slaying of something" (1985, p. 150), most often the dragon, which is a personification of the instinctual psyche. "Outbursts of affect, resentment, pleasure, and power demands—all these must undergo *mortificatio* if the libido trapped in primitive, infantile forms is to be transformed" (ibid.). The brainstem is considered the seat of instinctual functions and primitive emotions. Through the surgery on Jürg's brainstem, it was as though symbolically the devil had been released and made his unexpected appearance in my painting, announcing the danger inherent in such a delicate procedure and its aftermath. From that perspective, I had been right to denounce the tumor as the devil. During the course of recovery, we would have to suffer multiple stages of *nigredo* and *mortificatio* (the hellfire), to which later paintings attest.

Painting 3
Painting 3 is the second painting completed in the many hours of my vigil during the operation. Whereas the first one is dominated by violent outbursts of red and orange, this one is held in subtle hues of blue, green, and gold, conveying the sense of resolve and peace I had felt. The color black, a property of the devil in the previous painting, is now spread as an island on which the two figures are kneeling. Their postures and faces are downcast and

reflective. As in the previous painting, they appear to represent the couple. Here, the man is on the right side and the woman on the left, but this time they have turned their backs toward each other: they are in different worlds. In the background the large head of the horned animal, a cow, is situated between the two people, her body extending to the man's side. Perhaps he is even straddling the cow's back and looking toward her hindquarters, the locus of her generative and nurturing forces. The female figure looks pregnant, and her pregnant belly is on the same level as the cow's head. A sweeping, egg-shaped semicircle connects the man's neck with the woman's belly, as if there was an intimate connection between the two. The orange shape has not been worked out. It looks a bit like a felled tree, with one root sticking into the air. Or it could be imagined as the beam of a large scale or a seesaw, where the pregnant belly holds the middle of the orange beam that is tipped toward the woman's side.

Technically, this painting shows a variation in the treatment of the paint blot. Although the central fold creates two even sides, each side is treated differently, enhancing the notion that husband and wife are in different worlds. In circumstantial reality, Jürg had still been under the knife and under anesthesia, his spirit wandering in unknown dimensions, while I had been sitting on the floor in the surgeon's office.

The poem evokes the rainbow again, here in reference to the blue arch. Pictorially, it is as far removed from a real rainbow as was the black arch in the first painting. Symbolically, however, it is pregnant with meaning, like the woman in the painting. The rainbow is "rising," which may indicate a lifting of spirit and of hope. Moreover, it bridges the one who contemplates the past and the one who looks toward the future. In the poem, I did not refer to my husband as the one looking toward the future while I am contemplating the past (as had been our typical attitudes in life). Rather, I conceived of the two figures as two perspectives, perhaps of myself. In ever so many subtle ways, here and as evident in later paintings (number 12, for example), my imagination anticipated an imminent reversal of roles.

The rainbow, at one end touching the area of the back of the man's neck (exactly where Jürg's tumor had resided) and at the other the woman's belly, makes a meaningful connection between outer life circumstances and my inner process. It illustrates how Jürg's acute illness and operation had been the reason for me to become symbolically pregnant. Something new was stirring in my psyche; a new form of life wanted to be born. The blue arch contributes to the same idea. Cutting out an oval, egg-shaped or womblike, it opens up into the universe with its spinning galaxies. This perhaps influenced the poem's pronouncing, "what was below will be above," reminiscent of the statement in the famous alchemical text, *Tabula Smaragdina* (Henderson and Sherwood 2003, p. 10). I, up to now the follower ("below"), would eventually have to become the leader ("above"), the head of household who makes decisions and takes responsibility for the welfare of the family.

The cow takes center stage in the picture, her head turned toward us, looking us straight in the eye. She is a strong presence, sovereign and seemingly unmoved, her gaze steady as if saying: "I am the One—I am who I am." Although I had carefully outlined her features in the painting, I would not acknowledge her in the poem at all. The cow truly just *is*. Of course, in the culture and landscape of Switzerland, the cow is omnipresent; cows are a given, quite as I treated her in the painting. Because agriculture and urban life were (and perhaps to a lesser degree still are) so closely woven into each other, people were never very far from cows, stables, grass, and manure. Many old customs revolve around the cow and hundreds of gift items and souvenirs bear her image. In the mountainous regions, the early summer ascent of the cows from the valley to the alpine meadows and their return in the fall are celebrated events. Yet, unlike in India, the cow in Switzerland has only practical—if sentimental folkloric—significance and no mythic or religious ramifications.

The reverence for the cow in India harks back to the ancient agrarian matriarchal cultures, when archetypal feminine significance was attributed to the milk-giving cow; according to Neumann, she became the foremost representation of the Great Mother in her life-giving and sustaining aspect. Neumann notes, "the Goddess as cow, ruling over the food-giving herd, is one of the earliest historical objects of worship, occurring among the Mesopotamian population after the al'Ubaid period" (1955, p. 124). In Sumer, the great cow was depicted as a crescent moon, and in ancient Egypt, the cow Ahet was the origin of all manifestations and mother of the sun (Chevalier and Gheerbrant 1969). One of the most frequently reproduced figures is a bronze statue from the last millennium BCE of Isis as the great cow goddess, "wearing a headdress of the sun between cow-horns, suckling the child-king Horus and acting as his throne" (Husain 1997, p. 32; see also Neumann 1955, plate 44, and Woodman and Dickson 1969, p. 20). She was most revered as Mother Hathor, the heavenly cow, whose udder produced the Milky Way, whose body was the firmament, and who daily gave birth to the sun, Horus-Ra, her golden calf. Moreover, as Walker notes, "the Cow as creatress was equally prominent in myths of northern Europe, where she was named Audumla; she was also Freya, or a Valkyrie taking the form of a 'fierce cow'" (1983, p. 181).

But the heavenly cow also had a devouring aspect. The Egyptian Hathor, the good cow goddess, for example, becomes the goddess of the underworld in the form of a hippopotamus (Neumann 1955). Thus, in the image of the cow, the Great Goddess makes her appearance in this third painting, although unacknowledged as yet. Symbolically, the one figure (who could be Jürg), straddling the cow's back and looking toward an uncertain future, is given over to her power—for better or for worse.

From the perspective of alchemy, as I view it, the imagery in this painting pertains to the stage of *separatio*. The devilish tumor has burst the couple asunder; now man and woman are separated and turn their backs to each other. Edinger, who relates *separatio* to creation myths that begin with a separation of the original undivided One into two parts (like heaven and earth), points to the importance of space opening up. Psychologically, he maintains, it signifies the creation of the first pair of opposites and therefore represents the birth of consciousness: "Space for consciousness to exist appears between the opposites, which means that one becomes conscious as one is able to contain and endure the opposites within" (1985, p. 187). From this perspective, the value of my imaginal paintings lay precisely in using the space that had opened up between myself and my husband, through the sudden illness, for the opening and re-creation of my inner psychic world in a unique way. Edinger's comment that "swords, knives and sharp cutting edges of all kinds belong to the symbolism of *separatio*" (ibid., p. 191) is sadly ironic here, in that the separation was literally initiated by a surgical knife in a real operation: cutting through flesh and bones. It makes sense, in this case, that *separatio*, like *solutio*, is closely related to the aspect of *mortificatio*— representing the "killing" of the oneness in which husband and wife were well contained in one another and the pain involved in breaking up the old inner and interpersonal structures that had been working well.

Another aspect associated with *separatio* is the alchemical *extractio*, which has to do with "the extraction of meaning or psychic value from a particular, concrete object or situation" (Edinger 1985, p. 202). Indeed, in an acute crisis it may be a matter of psychological survival to extract meaning and psychic value, which I found through my ongoing imaginal process. In the particular transition from the second to the third painting—in the hours of anxious waiting in the surgeon's office—I had been able to separate myself from my angry feelings and extract a new perspective that included sadness and a kind of resignation, expressed in the color scheme proceeding from red to blue and yellow. In Hillman's view, the alchemical blue brings the black from the underworld with it (so visible in the black island in my painting), that is, the *nigredo* and *mortificatio*, depression and sadness of the soul, expressed now-adays as "having the blues." Hillman quotes Pseudo-Dionysius, who says that images painted blue "show the hidden depth of their nature" (2010, p. 105). Blue is the traditional color of the Virgin's celestial cloak, "she is the earth covered by the blue tent of the sky" (Jung 1940, par. 123). Hillman understands "the Jungian notion of blue as 'the thinking function,' to refer to blue's ancient association with the impersonal depths of sky and sea, the wisdom of Sophia, moral philosophy and truth" (2010, p. 105). Then again, he observes that

> evidently, the blue streaks and blue flames of celestial aspirations require a modicum of depression, a drop of putrefaction. A degree of darkness is the saving grace of inspiration. *In fact, the saving grace of Mary's light blue may lie in an imperceptible black Madonna cloaked within her robe.* (Ibid., pp. 104–105, emphasis added)

The alchemical yellow, often used as a synonym for gold, symbolizes "light, value, consciousness" (Edinger 1985, p. 161), and according to Dorn, "signifies the intellect, the principal 'informator' (formative agent) in the alchemical process" (Jung 1955–56, par. 390). Essentially, gold is best known as the goal of the alchemical opus. In the work of philosophical alchemists, it figures as "our gold" (*aurum nostrum*), which is not ordinary (*non vulgi*) but philosophical (*philosophicum*) gold. It is the inner sun (*Sol*), the center, akin to Jung's notion of the Self. Jung points out, however, that probably owing to its all too obvious analogy with the sun, "gold was denied the highest philosophical honour, which fell instead to the *lapis philosophorum*. The transformer is above the transformed, and transformation is one of the magical properties of the marvelous stone" (1952b, par. 99).

There is a plate in the *Splendor Solis* portraying the queen, or muse, in the alembic (see Henderson and Sherwood, p. 146). She is held entirely in blue and gold tones, wrapped in a pale blue robe, wearing golden adornments, surrounded by a blue and yellow band and standing on a golden platform showing a man's profile. Yet although this queen and the woman in my painting share the same color scheme with its symbolic implications, a whole alchemical opus lies between the two: the queen in the alembic marks the *quintessence*—the attainment of the goal and completion, whereas the woman kneeling on a black island is still at the beginning of the work. Fitting, therefore, is the designation of the golden sun in my poem as "shining *from the future.*"

Painting 4

This paint blot has a vertical and a horizontal fold — a small technical variation, thereby creating a double symmetry. The horizontal line marks a very distinct division into an above and below, an upper world and a lower world. Each is treated differently. The lower world suggests the watery element, whereas the upper world, with its colorful hills and mountaintops, belongs to earth and air. The faint impression of glaciers in the background heightens the sense of far-off distances and eternally remote heavens. In this field, the dried paint readily suggested the plumage of a large bird, with hardly a need to emphasize the feathers of the wings at all. Given the round shape of its head, it naturally became an owl. It flies toward us and stares directly and intently at the viewer, as if to convey an important message. It has an almost hypnotic effect. The turtle below also came into existence with minimal finishing touches; only the shell, head, and feet had to be outlined a bit. The eye, I believe, had been there as is. The turtle seems to be resting on something dark, deep down in the underworld, which looks like the mushroom cloud created by an erupting volcano, or even the explosion of an atomic bomb. These are disturbing asso-ciations, reminiscent of the dream that opens my story. They must be appro-priate for a "blow of fate" that is disruptive, even potentially destructive, to the life of the ego. Yet the turtle is seemingly unconcerned, gazing sideways at us with an almost humorous expression.

The poem tells how the appearance of Owl and Turtle came like a surprising gift that moved me to the core of my being, prompting the spon-taneous, heartfelt invocation. It was one of those moments when imaginal figures (whether from a dream or active imagination) *look at us* — in this case, straight in the eye — and not just we at them. Owl and Turtle had allowed me to acknowledge how small and helpless I really felt. It was safe to cry out to them, and they rewarded me with a felt sense of psychic energy streaming through me that translated into physical wellbeing, too. What I read in Owl's eyes, at the time, was a promise that I didn't have to feel abandoned. And on some level, though not expressed, there also had been a sense that I had to look the ordeal unflinchingly in the eye. Turtle, in turn, looked so entirely unconcerned on that black "thing," as if to convey a basic trust even in the darkest moments of life.

At one point in my studies I came across a statement from Jung, used as an epigraph in a book (Veronica Goodchild's *Eros and Chaos*), that struck me immediately as fitting my situation: "It is . . . only in the state of complete abandonment and loneliness that we experience the helpful powers of our own natures."[10] Such had been, indeed, my experience at the time: I had immediately perceived these animals in their archetypal feminine nature (aided by their female gender in German), coming from the heights and depths of the planetary psyche as "helpful powers" and welcomed them with an open heart.

In my poem, I emphasized a present-day, general symbolic meaning of these animals: wisdom and longevity. Yet the owl and the turtle are imbued with particularly rich symbolism in reference to the ancient Great Goddess, and, in my research, much of it has come to my surprise—as surprising as their appearance in the paint.

The owl has stirred the imagination of peoples from time immemorial. Some of the very oldest representations of the primordial Great Goddess were in the guise of owls. Gimbutas shows engravings of three snowy owls from the Upper Paleolithic cave known as the "Gallery of Owls" (13,000 BCE), pointing out that today's ambivalent image of this bird is only "a dim reflection, diffused through time, of the owl as incarnate manifestation of the fearsome Goddess of Death" (1989, p. 191). But Gimbutas is adamant in pointing out that there is much more emphasis on regeneration than on death in the iconography, as demonstrated, for example, by the pottery urns from the Bronze Age in the form of owls. They show "the universal Owl Goddess's face and breasts," with the aspect of regeneration emphasized "by large vulvas or serpentine umbilical cords" (Gimbutas 1989, p. 191, figure 292). In Mesopotamia, the owl goddess was known as Lilith, whose name means "screech owl." She was the goddess of night, evil, and death, depicted "winged, bird-footed, and accompanied by owls" (Neumann 1955, p. 272). A very early representation of the owl goddess has been called the eye goddess; the relation of owl goddess to eye goddess makes sense given the placement of the owl's eyes (see Gimbutas 1989, pp. 54–55). A reproduction of an alabaster figurine from 2,500 BCE is not easily forgotten (Neumann 1955, plate 87). With her eerily staring eyes, strange smile, and large hat, she looks rather like a Halloween witch. Then again, the owl's association with witches is well known, as Walker notes: "One of the medieval names for the owl was 'night hag'; it was said to be a witch in bird form" (1983, p. 754). Witches, in turn, have an ancient tie to Hecate, the awesome triple moon goddess. In folklore, the owl is richly endowed with legend and superstition.

A nocturnal bird that hunts its prey by night, characterized by its uncanny hooting, it is an omen "portending misfortune or heralding death" (Matthews 1978, p. 143). The attribute of wisdom derives from its very appearance, seemingly pensive and brooding. Its eyes that can see in the dark enable it to penetrate, symbolically, "the darkness of ignorance." Athena, the Greek goddess of wisdom and learning, had a companion owl on her shoulder that revealed unseen truths to her. The owl had the ability to light up Athena's blind side, enabling her to speak the whole truth, as opposed to only a half-truth. The owl in my painting, then, with her whitish and grey plumage, apparently coming from far-off glaciers, could well be a snowy owl. But at the time, I did not know about her as a harbinger of death, nor would I have been ready to receive "the whole truth." Quite to the contrary, I took Owl and Turtle as a sign that life would extend into wise old age for both Jürg and myself.

Turtle has an equally impressive symbolic history. In association with the Great Goddess, the turtle, like the owl, is honored in its nocturnal and lunar symbolism. In post-Paleolithic prehistory, the turtle was also an eminent symbol of regeneration. Gimbutas writes: "As the promoter of the beginning of the life cycle, the Goddess appears as a tiny mysterious fetus or a uterus-like animal—the frog or toad, lizard, turtle, hare or hedgehog, and fish" (1989, p. 185). In myths and legends, the turtle or tortoise is nothing less than a figure representing the universe or, as in some Native American myths, instrumental in the creation of the earth, given its form that comprises "a whole cosmography in itself with its shell, the upper half curved like the Heavens . . . and the lower flat like the Earth" (Chevalier and Gheerbrant 1969, p. 1916).

While revisiting the paintings, a potential third animal figure has suddenly revealed itself to me, lingering in the watery purple-blue color that surrounds the turtle: a large, crouching rabbit facing to the left. Its head with mouth, nostril, and eye can easily be made out. It is important to recognize it here, for the rabbit, as mythic Hare, may represent the masculine principle (and has masculine gender in German). Like the horned animal in the first painting, it is immersed in the watery element and was met with similar treatment at the time of painting—it was overlooked; it remained incognito. Yet in archetypal symbolism, the hare partakes in a similar way to the Horned God in the lore surrounding the ancient goddess:

> In that tapestry which serves as the backcloth to deep dream-states
> and on which the archetypes of the world of symbols are depicted,
> it is essential to bear in mind the vast importance of animals con-
> nected with the Moon, . . . like the Moon, hares and rabbits are
> linked to that oldest of deities, the Earth Mother, to the symbolism

of water which makes fruitful and regenerates, of plants and of the constant renewal of life in all its shapes. This is the world of that great mystery of life renewed through death. (Ibid., p. 472)

The hare is often the accomplice or close relative of the moon goddess. An endearing testimony of their intimate relationship is preserved in a sculpture from about 800 CE. The Mayan goddess Ixchel and Hare are portrayed as having equal stature, kneeling closely next to each other in a meditative attitude, Hare with his arm slung across the goddess's neck (see, for example, Austen 1990, p. 51; also on the Internet, search for "Ixchel"). The Maya-Quiché believed that the goddess was helped and saved by a hero rabbit when in danger. "Rabbits—or, more frequently, hares—thus become culture-heros, Demiurges or mythic ancestors" (Chevalier and Gheerbrant 1969, p. 472). Especially impressive is Menebuch, the great hare of the Algonquin Ojibwa and Sioux Winnebago, who serves as "intercessor between this world and the transcendent realities of the Otherworld" (ibid., p. 473). Therefore, he is considered an emblem of the lunar messiah, in contrast with the conquering and solar warrior or, as Neumann puts it, "an archetypal symbol of self-sacrifice" (1955, p. 199n). Henderson quotes Radin, who distinguishes four distinct cycles in the hero myth: "the Trickster cycle, the Hare cycle, the Red Horn cycle, and the Twin cycle" (1983, p. 112). Menebuch is an archetypal expression of the second cycle. He is still animal, "but all the same he appears as the founder of human culture—the Transformer" (ibid., p. 113). In the Hare cycle, "the culture-hero is a weak yet struggling figure, *ready to sacrifice childishness for the sake of further development*" (ibid., p. 118, emphasis added). I emphasize Henderson's interpretation because it succinctly points to what I suggest had been going on in the deep unconscious of my psyche.

For the alchemists, the tortoise evidently was an "instrument," symbolizing the instinctual side of the unconscious. Chevalier and Gheerbrant mention a woodcut in the famous Renaissance book, *Hypnerotomachia Poliphili*, showing the same symbolism contained in my painting (1969, p. 1018). The woodcut supposedly depicts a woman who holds a tortoise in one hand and pair of spreading wings in the other. Its "patently hermetic symbolism . . . [contrasts] the chthonian and celestial properties represented respectively by the tortoise and the wings" (ibid.). The authors point out that the Chinese alchemists regarded the tortoise as the beginning of the spiritualization of matter, its goal symbolized by the wings, quoting one alchemical text that calls the tortoise "a deadly poison before it was prepared and a sovereign antidote afterward. With it, Mercury gained such infinite wealth as the Philosopher's Stone obtains" (ibid.).

It appears, therefore, that the fourth painting contains, far beyond my conscious knowing at the time, a hermetic image that symbolically lays out the alchemical opus (and, in Jung's terms, the potential for an individuation process): the tortoise below and the (owl) wings above.

Painting 5

Paradoxically, imagining Jürg as a patient in the hospital became more real and taxing than if I had been physically there with him. My painful feelings translated into an image burning with diffuse shades of red, orange, and yellow, intensified by the two flaming torches on either side (the one on the left cut off in part when the photocopy was made). A palm tree occupies the center of the painting. It is tall, sturdy, and spreading its branches wide, imagined as extending above into the sky and below into the ground. The picture suggests a shaded oasis, where the tired traveler finds refuge from the glowing, hellish heat of the desert.

The emphasis here is on the two axes themselves, the vertical and the horizontal, so that the shape of an even-handed cross is brought out. The vertical axis is represented by the palm tree, whereas the horizontal axis is a thin line that upholds a burning torch on either side. The line widens into a central diamond-shaped field of purple color in the middle of the palm tree, with two of its corners hidden behind its trunk and the other two located on the axis.

Similar to the previous painting, the poem is an invocation. In my imagination the two burning torches are "lights of the eyes" (*Augenlichter*), and I call upon them to focus their luminosity on the third, represented by the diamond shape in the center. At the time, the image had been symbolic of a particular meditative state I had experienced often in our Zen practice: accessing a certain central point of deep concentration would allow one to transcend all physical, mental, emotional, and spiritual discomfort one might have during a sitting. It is the paradox of going farther into the pain as the way out of it. This, then, is the palm of victory, the transcendence to another realm beyond pain—a state that I had so ardently wished for my husband and also for myself. Coleman (1997) describes a similar experience in his shamanic journey. While undergoing a difficult operation and subsequent painful recovery only the complete focus and concentration onto a small, bright light dancing before his eyes brought relief from post-surgical pain.

My poetic association of a burning torch with the human eye evidently has its template in old mystic and mythical traditions. The Egyptian sun god Ra, for example, "was endowed with a burning eye, which was a symbol of his fiery nature" (Chevalier and Gheerbrant 1969, p. 364). In Becker's encyclopedia of symbols I came upon a little drawing made after a mural in an Egyptian grave, depicting the eye of Horus holding a torch. The torch, as a concentrated form of fire, is "a common symbol of purification and enlightenment in rites of initiation," its light illuminating the passage through the underworld (1992, p. 200). In antiquity, the downward-pointed torch was a symbol for the extinguishing of life. A search further back in history yields a rich harvest of symbolic associations that link the torch with the Great Goddess. It once was a prominent attribute of the fearsome triple moon goddess in her personification as "Hecate the Three-headed" (Harding 1935, p. 113). In that form, the goddess is a composition of Artemis, Selene, and Hecate, representing the moon in its three phases: Artemis is the crescent or waxing moon, Selene the full moon, and Hecate the waning and dark moon. According to Neumann, Hecate is the mother goddess in her devouring aspect as earth, night, and underworld. Images show Hecate with three heads and three pairs of arms. On an engraved gem, her arms are outstretched; the uppermost pair holds knives, the middle pair whips, and the lowest pair burning torches—all instruments intended to inflict pain and suffering for the sake of purification and transformation (see Neumann 1955, p. 169). In a more benign version, the Hecaterion of Marienbad, four of the six arms hold upright torches, the other two a pitcher and a plate (see Harding 1935, frontispiece). This version might be a vestige of the prehistoric goddess, who was not only destroyer but also nurturer and regeneratrix. Hecate was feared. Jung describes her as "a real spook-goddess of night and phantoms, a nightmare" (1952c, par. 577). Still, to the extent that she was perceived to be a disturbing influence in the inner world, responsible for lunacy, she was also recognized as "Sender of Nocturnal Visions" (Harding 1935, p. 114). In this context, the torches symbolize illumination.

> A legend tells the story of how Orestes brought the worship of the
> Goddess to Italy by carrying her image concealed in a bundle of
> faggots. In Italy they named her Diviana, which means *The* Goddess,
> a name that is more familiar to us in its shortened form of Diana . . . .
> She is shown in her statues crowned with the crescent and carrying

a raised torch. The Latin word for torch is *vesta*, and Diana was also known as Vesta [keeper of the hearth]. (Ibid., p. 130)

Diana was represented as the "Many-Breasted," sometimes white and sometimes dark-skinned (ibid., p. 108; see also Neumann 1955, plate 35). Her main festival was called the Festival of Torches, on August 15, when her grove was illuminated by a multitude of torches. Centuries later, the Catholic Church dedicated the date as a Festival of Candles to the Virgin Mary, and it became the day of her assumption. The dark image of the goddess has persisted in some of the Virgin's representations, and to this day representations of the Black Madonna in Europe are sought out for their wonder-workings and healing powers, often regarded as more effective than white representations of the Virgin.

The triple goddess in her dark aspect as queen of the underworld is associated with hell. Yet only in Christian times did hell become a fiery purgatory for sinners, the domain ruled by the devil. The word *hell* itself was borrowed from the Norse queen of the underworld, Hel, who sometimes wore all three faces of the triple goddess. But the ancient, matriarchal "hell" had significance as a uterine shrine, a sacred cave of rebirth (Craze 1969).

These amplifications, linking hellish suffering with the goddess's power of regeneration, with initiation and illumination through a descent into the underworld, certainly give deeper resonance and meaning to an illness. Unfortunately, New Age spirituality has contributed to the idea that serious illness, especially cancer, must be a sign of spiritual failing. Dyane Sherwood (1997), speaking from personal experience, argues eloquently against the propagation of this notion, which has often proven devastating for the afflicted, as well as for the people relating to them.

In my poem, I refer to the "palm of victory." In the history of the Olympic Games, both torch and palm play a role. There, however, the victory palm is just a branch or a wreath, whereas in my painting it is a very tall and sturdy tree, wonderfully soothing, a quality inherently true of the palm tree—once an ubiquitous image of the Great Mother in her nurturing aspect. Especially in Egyptian art, the goddess as sycamore or date palm, providing nourishment for the souls, is a central figure. Neumann writes:

As a fruit-bearing tree of life it is female: it bears, transform, nourishes. The protective character is evident in the treetop that shelters nests and birds. But in addition the tree trunk is a container, 'in' which dwells its spirit, as the soul dwells in the body. (1955, p. 49)

The tree goddess is both nurturing and generative; in Egyptian mythology, the top of the tree is the place where she gives birth to the sun. The symbol would suggest that honoring the archetypal feminine embodied in the vegetation generates a new consciousness.

The spirit of the palm tree as the Great Mother was still alive in the tradition of early Christians, who gave the title of Holy Palm (Ta-Mari) to the Virgin Mary. There is an illustration in Jung's *Psychology and Alchemy* depicting the Virgin surrounded by her attributes, "the quadrangular enclosed garden, the round temple, tower, gate, well and fountain, palms and cypresses (trees of life), all feminine symbols" (1952b, par. 92 and fig. 26).

In this painting, the juncture of the "beneficial" and the "terrible" aspects of the archetypal feminine (symbolized on the vertical and the horizontal axes, respectively) is emphasized by the purple, diamond-shaped field, which I had imagined as the "third eye." Chevalier and Gheerbrant note that in Eastern religions the two eyes are identified with the two luminaries, sun and moon, as a pair of opposites (as in alchemy). Resolving the duality requires a transition from a perception that discerns to a perception that unites and synthesizes. This, then, is the function of the third eye:

88

> This is the "Eye of Wisdom" . . . which is set on the bounds of unity and multiplicity, of emptiness and non-emptiness and is therefore able to perceive them simultaneously. It is, in fact, an organ of inward vision, and, as such, an exteriorization of the "eye of the heart." (Chevalier and Gheerbrant 1969, p. 363)

The diamond represents supreme qualities of spirit, similar to the third eye. It is associated with enlightenment, immortality, true Buddha nature, and immutability. Several of these elements come together in my poetic imagination. The diamond's immutability is described as "above all an *'axial'* characteristic," which is why "the Buddha's throne, set at the foot of the Bodhi-tree [symbolizing the World Axis], is a diamond throne" (ibid., p. 290, emphasis added).

Jung, in his alchemical studies, frequently refers to the importance of "the diamond body" in Chinese alchemy. As he points out in his "Commentary on 'The Secret of the Golden Flower,'" the treatise contains "a sort of alchemical instruction as to the method or way of producing the 'diamond body'":

> If thou wouldst complete the diamond body with no outflowing,
> Diligently heat the roots of consciousness and life.
> Kindle light in the blessed country ever close at hand,
> And there hidden, let thy true self always dwell. (1957, par. 28–29)

In an annotation, Jung remarks that in this text "human nature" and "consciousness" are used interchangeably (ibid., n3). What is meant in the above passage is the birth of a "superior personality" (ibid., par. 68), also known as "the incorruptible breath-body which grows in the golden flower or in the 'field of the square inch'" (ibid., par. 76), comparable to Jung's notion of the Self and the alchemists' philosopher's stone.

As with the previous painting, I found an alchemical illustration that combines the aspects that are present in my painting in an allegorical image. It is depicted in Jung's *Psychology and Alchemy* as "an illustration from the Ripley treatise" and shown enlarged in Neumann, where it is said to come from a Swiss manuscript, sixteenth century (1952b, par. 499 and fig. 231; Neumann 1955, plate 110). The image shows a naked woman standing on two conjoint alchemical ovens, with distillation jars on either side. In each hand, she holds a burning torch, facing downward. Her body is a tree trunk. From her crowned head sprout three branches with many twigs full of leaves, fruits, and birds flying to and fro. One large bird with outspread wings is poised in the center, standing on her head. There are effigies of the sun on the right side of the woman's head and of the moon on the left. This is "Mercurius as virgin (Pandora) and *arbor philosophica*" (Jung 1952b, par. 499 and fig. 231).

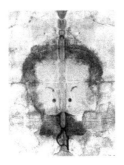

Painting 6

This painting has a similar palette as the previous one, and it is thematically related as well. I view it as a development of the former. There, the theme of suffering was expressed through universal symbols of elemental and plant life, whereas now it has taken on human and personal features. The physical discomfort and psychological suffering apparently had reached a peak. I had participated in both—vicariously, to be sure, but in a husband-and-wife union, the attending partner's pain has its own reality.

In this picture, the longer fold is used as the vertical axis. Most likely, I had folded the paper lengthwise first, given that the green paint had blotted only in the area of the lower part. Within the dark gray ring there must have been some dot here and little smear there to suggest eye and brow, and thus the face came into existence. It is a man's face, with black hair, moustache, and beard, the round, narrowly set eyes giving it a rather crazed expression. The image is a symbolic approximation of reality, of Jürg in the hospital. His face was still disfigured by the plastic tubes coming out of nose and mouth, held in place with tape, which did make him "crazy." The painting, in fact, was kinder than the reality; it transformed these tubes into a tuberous plant. Its long stem grows straight up from what looks like a bulb below the man's mouth; it reaches above his head where it bursts into a blue double-blossoming flower.

In the previous painting, I had associated the intersection of the two axes surrounded by the diamond-shaped field with the third eye. It is remarkable that this intersection now happens to be situated exactly at the location of the third eye in the man's face. A yellow glow illuminates the area around it. In this spot, the theme of the previous painting—the intersection between suffering and enlightenment—is reiterated.

Plant life and greenery play a central role. It looks as though the man's face had sunken deep into the patchy, leafy greenery out of which the plant grows. For me, it became the image of my husband's "terrible vegetative state," his subhuman, hard-to-tolerate condition in his hospital bed. However, the painting symbolizes a process of transformation that grows organically from just within this environment of vegetation: the *real* plastic tubes are transformed into an *imaginal* living plant. The metaphor gives the man's face a transpersonal meaning.

As did the sturdy palm tree, the slender, long-stemmed double flower holds center stage. It could be a blue lotus blossom with many petals, resting on a three-petaled blue lily—two flowers endowed with rich archetypal symbolism. The botanical characteristics of the lotus have stirred Eastern peoples' mystical and worldly imagination. Chevalier and Gheerbrant write: "Blossoming on stagnant and murky waters with so sensual and imperious a perfection . . . it is easy to imagine the lotus as the very first sign of life upon the undifferentiated vastness of the primeval waters" (1969, p. 616). Indeed, the blossom grows out of the darkest area in the picture, which I had identified as the man's beard. Because the lotus closes and retires into the water at sunset, reemerging again at sunrise to open its petals, it is an ancient symbol of light out of darkness. These associations pertain to the promise contained in this painting for something new to be born from the vegetative state, for spiritual meaning to emerge, as indicated by the illuminated area around the third eye and by the blue flowers.

In an annotation, Jung mentions that the image of Buddha or Shiva in the lotus and of Christ in the rose (meaning in the womb of Mary) signifies "the seeding place of the diamond body in the golden flower" (1952b, p. 108, n11).

Jung thereby touches on symbolism that takes us back, once again, to the matriarchal goddess religions. In ancient Egyptian and in Asian cultures the lotus was the preeminent symbol for the goddess—and the "son of god" was originally the "son of the Goddess" (Neumann 1955, p. 241). To give just one example, the Tibetan goddess Tara, representing "sublime womanhood in the circle of the Buddhas and Bodhisattvas," is depicted with a book resting on a lotus blossom beside her shoulder as emblem of her illuminated wisdom (ibid., p. 333). Neumann notes:

> This illumination is no gift or flash of light fallen from heaven; it is a living growth, which has taken root in the moldering depths of the earth, which has grown slowly, fed by the numinous water of life, and put forth a closed bud that only in the end will open up a lotus blossom "in the unbroken light of heaven." (Ibid., p. 334)

Where the symbolic, transpersonal, or archetypal significance of the man in my picture is concerned, I have come to recognize his face, with his dense hair and beard, surrounded by greenery and with a plant growing from a bulb nestled in his beard, as an image of the Green Man. A rich palette of effigies and articles on the archetype is offered on Kathleen Jenks's website (www.mythinglinks.org). There are beautiful photos of the Green Man as he appears in stone carvings on the walls of churches in the British Isles and the rest of Europe: a man's burly face, immersed in foliage, with vines emerging from his mouth. In his article, Dan Noel (2002) surmises that the Green Man might be a Celtic survivor from a primeval past, indeed, a descendant of the Horned God. Meditating upon this figure "imaginatively, mythically, as a model of maleness," Noel attributes to the Green Man qualities similar to those Damery offers for the Horned God, suggesting that he represents "Dionysus's emotional attunement to his natural surround and to the women near him," as a counterpart to Apollo's distancing posture toward the earth:

> We have needed a Father Nature for a long time, and never more urgently than now, when all over the planet, armored men, in or out of uniform, terrorize each other, women and children, and what remains of the wildwood. (Noel 2002)

In my series of paintings so far, the Horned God has evolved from his secret presence as a horned animal in the first, to his appearance as the Christian devil in the second, to a simile of the Green Man in the sixth. Here, he is shown suffering in his "vegetative state," as if waiting for redemption—true for my husband's condition in the hospital as well as for "Father Nature," if seen from an archetypal, planetary perspective. In the process, he will undergo further transformations, in tandem with the presence and development of the goddess image.

Alchemy recognizes a green stage in the opus, the *viriditas*. According to Jung, it sometimes appears after the *nigredo* (1952b, par. 333). Abraham sums up its meaning as follows:

> Green in alchemy indicates that the matter in the vessel is in a state of unripeness, immaturity or youth, just as in nature green fruit is unripe fruit. Until the metal has been dissolved into its first matter or "prima materia," then purified and transmuted, it has not yet "ripened" into gold and is thus still green. Green is also the colour of verdigris on copper, a substance frequently linked with the disease or leprosy of metals which must be washed away so that regeneration may occur. (1998, pp. 90-91)

From a positive viewpoint, green in the alembic is a sign that the infant stone is animated and is growing to maturity. Abraham quotes the alchemist Philaletha, who wrote of the opus: "When you see the green colour, know that the substance now contains the germ of its highest life" (ibid.).

I view the patchy green in my painting to signify that the work is still "young"; the process has barely begun, and the emergence of the green is not far removed from the initial *nigredo*. The black is very much a presence in this picture. But according to the alchemical texts, we now can look for "a germ of the highest life." The following passage of Jung from the *Mysterium Coniunctionis* is, in an almost uncanny way, a description of my state at this point in the process:[11]

> The state of imperfect transformation, merely hoped for and waited for, does not seem to be one of torment only, but of positive, if hidden, happiness. It is the state of someone who, in his wanderings among the mazes of his psychic transformation, comes upon a secret happiness which reconciles him to his apparent loneliness. In communing with himself he finds not deadly boredom and melancholy but an inner partner; more than that, a relationship that seems like the happiness of a secret love, or like a hidden springtime, when the green seed sprouts from the barren earth, holding out the promise of future harvests. It is the alchemical *benedicta viriditas*, the blessed greenness, signifying on the one hand the "leprosy of the metals" (verdigris) but on the other the secret immanence of the divine spirit of life in all things. (1955–56, par. 623)

92

In the alchemical texts, there is an explicit connection between the spirit Mercurius, the Holy Spirit, and the figure of the green lion as both the cause and the essence of the "blessed greenness." Implicitly, there is also a symbolic connection to the Green Man, about whom Noel muses that he might well represent the *lumen naturae*, the "light of nature," or the spirit (Mercurius) concealed in matter.

The rose color that complements the green in my picture has a feminine connotation. The alchemists said that the green lion has rose-colored blood because of his close connection with Venus. The rosy color also refers to the rose as "a soubriquet of Mary" (Jung 1955–56, par. 419).

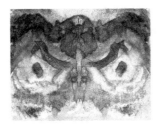

Painting 7

This painting is striking in its dense, colorful, and dynamic palette. All the colors of the rainbow are represented here; most conspicuously, a lively blue-purple spreads out in the form of a horizontal figure eight, infused by subdued reds, dotted by some green, and surrounded by deep golden yellow. Whereas the two black marks in the blue circles are unaltered, I had thickened the black band flowing along the upper edge quite a bit.

The thematic content has changed dramatically from the previous painting. Instead of earthy plant life, there are cosmic elements whirling; and instead of a tortured man's face, we now behold the image of a sweet child. Quietly smiling, it looks inward in deep meditation, its hands folded in prayer, which enhances the peaceful, meditative stance. This child has emerged as part of the vertical axis, seemingly floating in space, the folds of the dark red cape surrounding it like wings. But it also looks like it is immobilized, tightly held in place from its knees down by those round shapes. The child's praying hands also hold the reins, very loosely and gently, of the horses on either side. The child seems oblivious to them, and neither do I give any further regard to their presence in my poem. As with the cow in the third painting, the horses simply *are*, but in contrast to the stately and solid presence of the cow, these two horses seem fickle, and their appearance only makes a fleeting impression. It is as if they would quickly stick out their heads and necks (haggard and thin as is the child), only to vanish again from our sight.

I remember the felt sense of awe and wonder I had as the child emerged from the whirling elements. It was special; in the poem I had identified him as my "prince" (reminiscent, in his simplicity and genuineness, of Antoine de Saint-Exupéry's "Little Prince"), and in a deliberate action I had adorned him with a crown, which dramatically stands out from the dark background. In the small volume entitled *Essays on a Science of Mythology*, I found exquisite resonance to the symbolic image: Jung and Kerenyi's (1949) joint exploration of the child archetype and, as indicated in the subtitle, "the myth of the divine child." Jung notes, "the mythological idea of the child is emphatically not a copy of the empirical child but a symbol clearly recognizable as such: it is a wonder-child, a divine child, begotten, born, and brought up in quite extraordinary circumstances," and so, indeed, is my prince (ibid., p. 80, n. 21). The poem describes the fantasy I had spun about his extraordinary origins and circumstances. I surrounded him with what Kerenyi calls an "aura of fairytale" (ibid., p. 27): he emerges "out of water and fire's blaze / out of darkly clouded skies"; I find him "naked and haggardly thin" because he has been shivering in the cold for so long. These words suggest that he must have been abandoned and exposed to the elements, which is one of the most salient characteristics of child gods and (usually male) figures in heroic sagas: being abandoned at birth, orphaned, often threatened by and surviving extraordinary dangers. My painting also reflects Kerenyi's perception of the "*solitariness* of the child god, and the fact that he is nevertheless *at home in the primeval world*" (ibid., p. 28; emphasis added). My prince appears to be completely at peace alone and at home in the cosmos. Kerenyi, furthermore, points to the connection of the primordial child to the underworld through the water element, the primordial source of life, and this, too, fits my prince—uncannily so.

Once again, I find that the pictorial elements surrounding the prince, some developed, some not, are symbolic of the goddess as Great Mother in her dark, underworldly aspect. The grandest, in my view, is the face of Owl, as it is naturally present in the paint: the black spots within the blue fields are her eyes, staring at us, the wavy black ribbon perhaps suggesting the crown and her ears. The shape of a skull at the base of the little prince would represent Owl's beak. The skull also looks like the body of a red lobster, its shears pointing downward. Like the crab, it is an animal of the deep sea and belongs to the dark aspect of the goddess. The necks of the horses and the claws of the lobster form two sickles, one facing up and one down. The skull itself, wherein the legs and feet of the little prince are stuck, depict Kerenyi's observation that the child has a "kinship with the souls of the dead" (ibid., p. 69). Jung notes that the child motif often develops from pre-Christian sources, such as chthonic animals, for example. At other times, it appears "more cosmically" (ibid., p. 78). The image of my prince, and my imagining him as arising "out of water and fire's blaze," succinctly combine both aspects.

The horses, too, are eminent symbols of the triple moon goddess, linking "Earth and Mother, Moon and Water, sexuality and fertility, and plants and the rebirth of the seasons" (Chevalier and Gheerbrant 1969, p. 521). The following passage about the horse is a beautiful illustration of the same imagery:

> A belief, firmly seated in folk memory through out the world, associ-
> ates the horse in the beginning of time with darkness and with the
> chthonian world from which it sprang, cantering, like blood pulsating
> in the veins, out of the bowels of the Earth or from the depths of the
> sea. This archetypal horse was the mysterious child of darkness and
> carrier both of death and of life, linked as it was to the destructive
> yet triumphant powers of Fire and to the nurturing yet suffocating
> powers of Water. (Ibid., p. 516)

Hecate is portrayed riding a horse, and Demeter is sometimes depicted as a horse-headed goddess. In that conjunction, Jung provides a long etymological discourse on *nightmare, mare, mother, mar,* and so on. There seems to be an obvious connection between nightmare and mare (female horse), but the word *nightmare* goes back to Old English and Old Norse *mara*, "ogress, demon" — thus, "demon of the night" (1952c, par. 370). Jung also links horse with mother, arguing that "as a beast of burden it is closely related to the mother-archetype (witness the Valkyries that bear the dead hero to Valhalla, the Trojan horse, etc.)" (1934, par. 347). "Mar," which had been my nickname, unintentionally fits into the chain of associations. Jung observes that the phonetic connection between the German *Mar*, French *mere*, and the various words for "sea" (Latin, *mare*; German *Meer*; French, *mer*) are certainly remarkable, though etymologi-cally accidental. "May it perhaps point back," Jung asks, "to the great primor-dial image of the mother, who was once our only world and later became the symbol of the whole world?" (1946, par. 373). Of course, at the time of crisis, my function as a mother had been particularly burdened. I was not only the mother of my children; I was also asked to be especially motherly toward my husband. How interesting that I also became the imaginal adoptive parent of the little prince, committed to nurturing him as well.

As I see it today, the appearance of the prince in my active imaginations signifies a very important step in the process. This child is truly born, in Jung's words, "out of the womb of the unconscious, begotten out of the depths of human nature, or rather *out of living Nature herself*" (Jung and Kerenyi 1949, p. 89; emphasis added). Remarkably, it is the first image that I welcomed on its own terms, without any reference to my relationship with my husband. Jung's evaluation of the child archetype succinctly reflects my psychological condition at the time. He writes: "'Child' means something evolving toward independence. This it cannot do without detaching itself from its origins: abandonment is therefore a necessary condition, not just a concomitant symptom" (ibid., p. 87). The part of me that had been psychologically, intellectually, and spiritually dependent upon my husband, all the while supporting him on his journey, needed to move toward independence. The symbol of the child, Jung holds, represents the potential future:

> In the individuation process, it anticipates the figure that comes from the synthesis of conscious and unconscious elements in the personality. It is therefore a symbol which unites the opposites; a mediator, bringer of healing, that is, one who makes whole. (Ibid., p. 83)

The child is "equipped with all the powers of nature and instinct" (ibid., p. 89), which gives it the numinous character the figure of the little prince unquestionably exudes. It represents "the strongest, the most ineluctable urge in every being, namely the urge to realize itself" (ibid).

In myth, Jung points out, the child sometimes looks more like a child god (personifying the collective unconscious), at other times more like a young hero (representing a synthesis of the divine—that is, not yet humanized—unconscious and human consciousness), the latter signifying "the potential anticipation of an individuation process which is approaching wholeness" (Jung and Kerenyi 1949, p. 85). The little prince in my painting obviously had to assume the role of a hero, for, in my poetic imagination, I anticipated that he would show me "the direction he elected"; he would be able to tame "the powers" and lead me to "heaven's gate."

Here, then, the dynamic masculine principle, so far lingering unrecognized in the watery element of the foregoing paintings (the horned animal and the hare) makes his appearance in his mythic, numinous, human-godlike form—a positive animus figure with great potential.

For the alchemists, Jung writes, the archetype of the child god was embodied in "Mercurius reborn in perfect form (as the hermaphrodite, *filius sapientiae,* or *infans noster*)" (ibid., p. 77). It is the philosophical child or philosophical stone born indeed "from the union of Sol and Luna at the chemical wedding" (Abraham 1998, p. 148). In a meaningful coincidence, the child makes his appearance in painting 7 of my series, a prime number made up of four and three, traditionally symbolic of the feminine and the masculine, respectively.

What I expressed in a few poetic sentences about my little prince contains some of the essential elements of alchemy's philosophical child, who was equivalent to the alchemical stone. Abraham summarizes:

> During the conception and birth of the Stone the alembic is known as the womb or the bed of birth. The Stone is known as the orphan and the alchemist plays the role of the foster-parent. As Ruland noted, "The Chemical Philosophers find their infant ready formed by nature" . . . . During the cibation, the alchemist must gradually nourish the infant Stone with "milk" and "meat" (the white and red mercurial waters) so that it may become sweet and strong. When it has grown to maturity, this infant has the power to conquer all disease and transform all things to perfection. Arthur Dee wrote of the infant Stone's maturation into the spiritual warrior: "he will become a king, stronger than a king, and so stout in Battell, that he alone being a most powerful Conqueror, will obtain the Victory against ten thousand Enemies." (Ibid., pp. 149–150)

What a striking contrast, though, between this mythic child with its heroic task and the "children at play" in plate 3.2 of the *Splendor Solis* (Henderson and Sherwood 2003, p. 164)! The plate depicts a bunch of rambunctious, well-fed little children in a spacious, warm, and pleasant room, watched over by the mother sitting in the background. They are engaged in a variety of activities: running around with a pinwheel, riding a hobbyhorse, caressing each other, or playing a rough-and-tumble game as a threesome. Some are clothed, others naked, and they are completely absorbed in their play. These are happy, unburdened children who are at home in *this* world. The text for this alchemical picture reads: "Wherefore is this Art compared to the play of children, who when they play, turn undermost that which was uppermost" (ibid., p. 163). Henderson and Sherwood comment:

> Just as children need play for normal psychological development, so do adults in order to continue to grow psychologically. Often people suffering from disappointments in life can hardly wait to get back to the achievement program that they left behind. They need the advice given to them by this image: "Just try to play, or let play go on in your imagination." (Ibid., pp. 164–165)

The little prince in my image lacks the worldly feistiness and the unself-conscious ease in the company of others, which the children in the alchemical picture display. But even this mythic child might have had a playful influence on my solitary, secretive activity, as would become evident in the following pictures.

Painting 8

This is the third picture painted in the hospital (paintings 2 and 3 were made during the operation), and these three exclusively happen to portray the couple, Mar and Jürg. This one, unlike the others, has a more literal aspect to it. I was in actuality crouching on the floor next to the hospital bed while painting, Jürg lying above me. Nevertheless, this image includes a symbolic object representation; it, too, has a transpersonal dimension.

Where method is concerned, this painting is the first one in which I varied the technique applied so far of folding the paper through the vertical and/or horizontal middle only, thereby predictably creating a single or double symmetry. Although the central fold in painting 8 is very dominant, there are additional diagonal folds visible that are irregular. It is possible that the child awakened in the previous image had gently stimulated me on a subconscious level to experiment and explore new ways of playing.

A serene tranquility and a sense of stability emanates from the picture. The horizontal line firmly divides the upper from the lower world and lets the patient (Jürg) rest securely on his pillows. The bent-over body of the woman (Mar) displays her broad back like a solid rock that offers support. One has the impression that the situation is stable, perhaps on hold, while the healing energies are gathering.

There is a peculiar feeling of ancientness present in the image that bestows a numinous quality. The red and golden halos, illuminating the darker tones of purple and blues as if from an unknown source, resemble medieval Christian artwork. The patient's head shimmers in an eerie greenish-white patina that gives it the impression of an old skull. The woman, bent over vapors arising from an unknown source, appears to be involved in a ritual. Although the man and the woman are dwelling in separate environments, there is a connection through the barely visible rays (the diagonal folds in the paper) fanning out around her figure and converging in a focal point at approximately the location of his eye.

There are two mythopoeic elements in the picture that transpose Mar and Jürg in the ICU beyond a literal rendering into the imaginal realm. One is an attribute of his, and one is associated with her. The strange channel arising from the patient's chest gives the impression that he is connected with something beyond the frame of the picture—*the* beyond, one must surmise. Although seemingly originating from the heart and not from the navel region, it looks like a thick navel cord. Symbolically, I would think, the image suggests that Jürg had become an infant of the Great Mother—her presence so large it wouldn't fit into the frame of the painting. He is delivered into her care, but also exposed to her will, the one who governs the processes of life, death, and rebirth. The woman I associated with is characterized in the poem as "the wise one . . . bending . . . / over the healing vapors" arising from deep chasms. She is in deep meditation, concentrated on the healing effect of the vapors or perhaps waiting to receive a message from the gods. In that capacity, she evokes the Greek myth of Delphi. Diane Skafte suggests that we all carry in our deep psyches the notion of Delphi as an ancient sacred place:

> Delphi. The name is like no other. From classical times to the present, people have revered Delphi as the paragon of all oracle sites . . . . The priestess herself, enthroned upon a three-legged platform, eyes closed in trance, has inspired the imagination of writers and poets for thousands of years. Even though she uttered her last words over fifteen hundred years ago, we have never let her voice fade from memory. (1997, p. 65)[12]

In prehistoric times, Delphi was a site where the goddess was worshiped as Mother Earth under the name of Delphyne, the Womb of Creation, still evident from the etymological reference: "Delph means 'uterus,' and Delphos signifies both fish and womb (Henderson and Sherwood 2003, p. 5). "Eventually," writes Walker, "the patriarchal god Apollo took it over . . . claiming to have placed the Serpent [her son and consort Python] in his underground uterine cave, whence came the oracle's inspiration" (1983, p. 218). Walker also notes that "the original Delphic oracle first belonged to the abyssal fish goddess under her pre-Hellenic name of Themis, often incarnate in a great fish, whale, or dolphin (delphinos)" (ibid., p. 313).

The symbolic elements in this picture (the navel chord rising up from Jürg's chest or belly region and the rising vapors or fumes over which Mar is bent) are precisely the ones that suggest a particular alchemical operation. Edinger notes that elevating processes and "all images that refer to an upward movement" have to do with *sublimatio* (1985, p. 118). Sublimation is one of the operations by which the substance that makes up the *prima materia* is purified. It is often mentioned together with distillation. The ascending movement of the *sublimatio* translates a low substance into a higher form: "That which is inferior is changed into something superior (*inferus* below; *superus* above)" (ibid., p. 117). Gareth Roberts writes: "All alchemical processes were governed by the idea of improving or making matter more refined or subtle" (1994, p. 59). He mentions a passage by the alchemist Geber who recommends a series of bewildering alternations between the fixed and the volatile: "by means of sublimation, make the fixed stone volatile, and the volatile fixed, the fixed soluble, and again the soluble volatile, and then once more the volatile fixed" (ibid.). Edinger's comment on a painting by one of his analysands provides a fitting psychological interpretation to the alchemist's recommendation:

> Upward movement, *sublimatio*, brings sublime vision, spiritual
> clarity, and broad perspective but without body, weight, or power
> to affect what one sees. Downward movement, *coagulatio*, brings
> weight, substance, and effective reality-functioning. (1990, p. 25)

That is, the two movements balance each other out. Like the painting Edinger is commenting on, my picture contains both elements: the image shows Jürg connected through the navel cord with the otherworld, the upper world of the spirits, while solidly lying there as a patient in the hospital bed; Mar is depicted as bending low toward the ground, perhaps the underworld, from where the fumes arise. Yet her broad back is a testimony that the reality of the illness—the pain and discomfort of the body, the emotional intensity and suffering created by the crisis—weigh her down. Rather than flee, it coagulates.

In my poem, I describe the vapors as "healing," thereby attributing medicinal value. They are also imagined as scented fumes (*Düfte*), reminiscent of incense. The incense offering during the Catholic mass, Jung reminds us, originated from the ancient customs of sacrificial fires, which, at a later stage, were conceived as a spiritualized form of food offering. Incense "signifies a transformation of the sacrificial gifts and of the altar, a spiritualization of all the physical substances . . . . The vapor also suggests the sublimated body, the *corpus volatile sive spirituale,* or wraithlike 'subtle body'" (Jung 1954c, par.

319). Incense as a rising spiritual substance thus "implements and represents the ascent of prayer" (ibid.). As we know, the alchemists understood prayer as a meditation consisting of an internal dialogue with God (or one's good angel). Through such prayerful meditation, the alchemists believed that "yet more spirit will be infused into the stone, i.e., it will become still more spiritualized, volatilized, or sublimated" (Jung 1952b, par. 390).

Here, the various symbolic meanings elicited by the image of the wise woman in the picture converge. She is hovering over "healing vapors" in a prayerful or meditative attitude. It implies that the spiritual meaning arising from the imaginal work is healing; it is making her psychologically whole.

Notably, the alchemical *sublimatio* is not to be confused with Freud's principle of sublimation. In a letter, Jung points out the difference:

> It is not a *voluntary and forcible* channeling of instinct into a spuri-
> ous field of application, but an *alchymical transformation* for which
> *fire* and the black *prima materia* are needed. *Sublimatio* is a great
> mystery. Freud has appropriated this concept and usurped it for the
> sphere of the will and the bourgeois, rationalistic ethos. (Quoted in
> Edinger 1985, p. 118)

The alchemists distinguished between a lesser and a greater *sublimatio*. Edinger notes that "the lesser *sublimatio* must always be followed by a descent, whereas the greater *sublimatio* is a culminating process, the final translation into eternity of that which has been created in time" (ibid., p. 140). Evidently, my painting portrays a lesser *sublimatio*; as it turns out, the descent follows on its heels.

Painting 9

In this painting, the same faded, gray-greenish, skull-like patina that illuminated the patient's head in the previous painting is now spreading over the

entire background. The grayish black around the edges looks like tufts of smoke hanging in the hot air. A white dove flies down from somewhere as in a "crash-flight," traversing the vigorously burning fire seemingly with determination. In my poem, I expressed the inevitability of the act: the dove *must* go through the fire—there is no other way.

Here, my technique entered into a new phase. There is no middle fold anymore; instead, I used a number of diagonals, which work in this picture to give the impression of a sword having slashed the paper—as if to slash any sense of hope still lingering in the heart. However, these diagonal lines also outlined the body of the dove so perfectly that it simply had to be whitened a bit for enhancement.

The dove carries supreme symbolic importance in the Judeo-Christian mythology, most familiar as an image of the Holy Spirit, as an allegory for peace and purity, and thus it stands for "the sublimation of the instincts and, specifically, of the erotic instincts" (Chevalier and Gheerbrant 1969, p. 306). Jung defines doves as "emblems of innocence and of marital love" (1955–56, par. 205), and in an annotation, "also of gentleness, tameness, peacefulness (dove of Noah), simplicity (. . . DV: 'guileless as doves')" (ibid., n 350). As if that was not enough, the dove assumed special meaning in our personal lives, given that the family name Tauber, in German, signifies a male dove or pigeon. But when Sōen Nakagawi Rōshi had initiated me into the Sangha (the Zen community) with the name Zenkiu, "good dove," a complex began to spin around it. At the time, I vaguely resented the blessing, for it seemed to tap into the patriarchal Christian symbolism, not only implying humility and altruistic love, but also an attitude of submitting to God and to the men in my life and (happily reinforced by my husband) performing the duties of wife and mother with eagerness and dedication.[13]

Now, many years later, my research and feminist studies have led me to comprehend the symbolism of the dove in its broad and awe-inspiring significance. In antiquity, the bird was intimately associated with the great love goddesses of Asia Minor, India, Crete, and Greece: Ishtar, Astarte, and Aphrodite. Neumann provides an illustration depicting a stone relief that shows the winged figure of the Carthaginian goddess of heaven, Tanith; above her arches a rainbow, topped by a hand, while beneath her are two doves, "the typical bird symbols of the Great Goddess" (1955, plate 157b and p. 311). Walker reminds us that the dove was "Aphrodite's totem, the bird of sexual passion, symbolically equivalent to the yoni. In India too, the dove was *paravita,* the symbol of lust. Joined to her consort, the phallic serpent, the Dove-goddess stood for sexual union and 'Life'" (1983, p. 252). But as long as the archetypal goddess still held within her the opposites, Aphrodite was also the bringer of death and in that aspect was known as "Irene, Dove of Peace" (ibid., p. 253). Romans called her Venus Columba, Venus the Dove. Her catacombs, mausoleums, and necropolis were known as *columbaria,* literally the Latin word for dovecotes.

According to Gimbutas, the Great Goddess of prehistoric times in her appearance as a dove was one of the principal images of death. I suspect that it is the doves' cooing, so similar to the hooting of owls, that made these birds "prophetic birds, omens of death, and spirits of the dead" (Gimbutas 1989, p. 187). Also believed to be the reincarnation of the soul, small birds were often depicted in funeral places. Gimbutas notes that in Russian, "*golubec* means 'grave marker,' from *golub,* 'dove, pigeon'" (ibid.).

The meaning I intuitively extracted from my painting was an understanding of the deep spiritual crisis the illness had unleashed, comparable to a trial by fire, through which the Christian qualities symbolic of the good dove were severely tested. The pure, white goodness might not remain unblemished—indeed, the dove might well become "blackened," as it were. This dove, descending from above and about to fly through the fire is an image of descent. I am reminded here of two well-known and significant portrayals of a woman's descent as initiation: One is the ancient Sumerian myth of the descent of Inanna, written on clay tablets dating from around 3500 BCE, which only over the last few decades has come into our awareness through original translations and Jungian interpretations.[14] The other is the more familiar Greek myth of the rape of Persephone, preserved for posterity in the Homeric hymn to Demeter. I suggest that my position at the time represented a remarkable combination of the two myths. In its physical reality and psychological effect, Jürg's sudden and unexpected illness had more of a forced and vehement descent (like Persephone's), for which I had been completely unprepared. Yet through my daily active imaginations, I willingly undertook an imaginal descent, step by step (like Inanna's).

In alchemy, images of consumption by fire abound and belong to the *calcinatio* operation. Edinger points out that *calcinatio* has two parts, sensibly: one aspect is cremation, leading to "death and blackness of *mortificatio,*" associated with hell and the purgatory, the other a "whitening," drying process that brings about the *albedo* (1985, pp. 21–22). The descent into the underworld "must be made," states James Hillman, confirming my assertion in the poem (quoted in Marlan 2005, p. 78). Moreover, as Hillman reminds us, the alchemists made a distinction between white "as a name for the *materia prima* . . . when white refers to unworked innocence, . . . sweet, shy virginity, and the like, and the white of the *albedo,* a cooling, which results from violent tortures, long-suffering patience, and intense heat" (2010, pp. 128–129). The white dove in my picture doubtlessly will be blackened before cooling to a white ash. Somehow I had had a hunch that this was how it was supposed to be: whatever was left of the innocent, sweet, shy Swiss girl had to be purged in the fire of suffering through the consequences of the illness.

The beautiful new *Book of Symbols,* published by the Archive for Research in Archetypal Symbolism (ARAS), shows an alchemical illustration under the title "Dove" that struck me with its related symbolic imagery. It shows an alembic in which a white dove descends in a crash flight from above, similar to the dove in my picture—not into a fire, but into a black sediment. The results are the same, however. The caption reads:

> *Purgatio.* A pristine dove descends into dark waters, activating processes that will bring high and low together. From the alchemical manual *De sapientia veterum philosophorum.* 18th century. (Ronnberg and Martin 2010, p. 244)

In the *Splendor Solis,* between the seventh and eleventh plates, a development is depicted in conjunction with the image of the dove that adds further meaning to my painting. In the seventh plate, portraying the death of the old king and the emergence of the new, the youth holds in his left hand a golden apple with a white dove perched upon it, seen here as a symbol of innocence and purity. The eleventh plate shows the alchemist sitting in a circular tub, heated by a roaring fire in the furnace beneath. Poised on his head is a white dove in full splendor. Henderson and Sherwood comment:

> The white bird that we saw perched on the golden fruit of the youthful king (Plate I-7) now appears upon the head of an ordinary human being. What was formerly the wish of the adept to *transcend the limitations of material reality* has resulted paradoxically in a humble and embodied spiritual attitude. The man is not flying; rather, he remains sitting in the great iron cauldron, still suffering and being transformed. This alchemical symbol conveys that *the work done on the chthonic, or earthly, level* has released the white bird, which ascends—the reverse of the Christian dogma that spiritual enlightenment comes only from above through divine revelation, as symbolized by the white dove descending [in a foregoing figure]. (2003, p. 100; emphasis added)

One might argue that the white dove in my painting represents an aspect that had *wished* to transcend the limitations of material reality, especially in the situation we, as a couple, found ourselves in. This aspect, then, was forced to undergo *calcinatio*, the trial by fire, and to submit to the work done on the chthonic level of reality.

Painting 10

It appears that darkness has covered up the background's skull-colored patina of the previous picture. It spreads out from the denser black in the center toward the edges, where some of the pink and yellowish colors still shine through. Around the vertical axis, the paint coagulates into denser shapes, which, all by themselves, outline the two barren tree trunks, raising their amputated branches toward heaven. I had only added the facial features — sad, pensive faces — with which the tree trunks are personified. There is something elflike about these two sorrowful beings; they could be tree gnomes in the deep woods, conferring with each other, mourning together the fateful events of this world. Symbolically, they may again represent the couple: the face above with a moustache that of the man; the face below with softer features that of the woman.

My poetic association of the tree trunks to "the crosses at Golgotha" indicates that, at this stage, the descent into hell was under way; I was experiencing the dark night of the soul. The painting itself is a stark image of suffering, crucifixion, and dying, unmitigated by the life-affirming aspects of tree symbolism: there are no leaves, blossoms, or fruits, no sprouting greenery that would point to salvation or to rebirth. The poem attests that I had accepted the suffering, vicariously lived through the ordeal of my husband in the hospital and simultaneously experienced as a sacred presence in my own psyche.

The imagery taps into the collective unconscious, where the tree or tree trunk, the cross, and the significance of Golgotha (that is, crucifixion) share a symbolic relationship since ancient history. In the following passage from "The

Philosophical Tree," Jung brings these elements into a meaningful connection with each other. He writes:

> In this context of thought, where suffering and sadness play so great a role, it is not surprising that *the tree* was brought into connection with *the cross* of Christ. This analogy was supported by the old legend that the wood of the cross came from the tree of paradise. (1954b, par. 446)

Neumann spells out how the Christian myth-making and formation of legends integrated the life-death-rebirth symbolism of the goddess by establishing a relationship between the tree of knowledge in the garden of Eden and "the tree of life and death that is the Cross" (1955, p. 253). During the Middle Ages, the Catholic Church claimed that the True Cross was made of the same wood as the tree of life in the garden of Eden. Adam had carried it out of the garden, and thereafter it was preserved by the church patriarchs. The legends say that the cross was planted on the very spot where the tree of life once grew. Thus, it became "the Tree of the Cross, so that whence came death, thence also life might rise again" (quoted in Walker 1983, p. 189).

The palm tree in painting 5 was symbolic of the tree of life, the nurturing and protecting aspect of the Great Mother, an oasis in the desert. Conversely, this painting portrays the tree as an abode of death. Here, writes Neumann, "the character of the earth-womb . . . is combined with the all-encompassing wood," as the dead were hoisted into the treetops and carved-out tree trunks served as coffins (1955, p. 50). The wood, which in the form of a cradle or crib is the container of new life, becomes in the form of a coffin "the mother of death, the 'sarco-phagus,' devourer of flesh that encloses the dead" (ibid., pp. 243/244). According to Neumann,

> sacrifice and suffering are the prerequisites of the transformation conferred by her, and this law of dying and becoming is an essential part of the wisdom of the Great Goddess of living things, the goddess of all growth, psychic as well as physical. (Ibid., p. 252)

Long before Christ there were myths of sacrifice by hanging, in which the hero, in Neumann's words, was "offered up to the god in connection with the act of initiation performed by himself" (ibid., p. 251). Well known is the Germanic god Odin (Wotan) hanging from Yggdrasil, the tree of fate, so that he was known by names such as Hanging God or the Dangling One. Neumann writes:

Regardless of theological superstructures, the archetypal symbolism of the tree reaches deep down into the mythical world of Christianity and Judaism. Christ, hanging from the tree of death is the fruit of suffering, and hence the pledge of the promised land . . . . Like Dionysus, He is *endendros*, the life at work in the tree. And the tree of knowledge is identified with the tree of life and death that is the Cross. (Ibid., p. 252)

At first, there seems to be no redeeming aspect visible in the dark patterns of this image. But as I let my eyes move to the lower right quadrant, they come to rest on the face there. While painting, I only had to emphasize slightly—one eye a bit; the brow—to bring it out. For me, it became the face of the moon, which is why I surrounded it with the large waning sickle. "He" has his own thoughts (*der Mond denkt das Seine*), I wrote, while I am crying. There is no knowing, neither then nor now, what his thoughts were, but look-ing into that round face with the loving eye, we might wonder whether it isn't it the face of a benign, nurturing mother, watching quietly over her infant. Could that have been, after all, the life-affirming impulse we have been looking for, coming from the deep unconscious?

The moon is given masculine gender in German. Apparently, the Germans held on to the perception of the moon as the spirit in women, reaching back into primordial times, when "the magical-spiritual reality of the female group" in matriarchal societies focused on the figure of the moon as "Lord of the Women" (Neumann 1955, p. 295). Neumann refers to a "spirit-moon root," which he associates with the "transpersonal male principle" and therefore with "the masculine spiritual aspect of the Feminine"—an aspect so promi-nently figuring in the German romantic movement, inspired and lunatic at once (ibid., p. 298). In Esther Harding's historical account, the most primitive belief about the moon was as "a *presence* or a fertilizing influence" (1935, p. 84). As religious forms evolved, the moon eventually became a male god. Ancient kings were considered incarnations of the moon man, wearing headdresses with bullhorns, "emblematic of the horned moon" (ibid., p. 88). Imagined in relation with the cycles of the moon, the moon god represented the pattern of the dying and resurrecting gods: Osiris in Egypt, Dionysus in Greece, Christ in Christianity. The early moon gods were also the sons of the moon mother, "not only bestower of fertility upon woman, but also her guardian and protector" (ibid., p. 93). As patron of all of woman's activities, it is almost as though the moon god must himself be a woman in disguise, Harding muses, thus he is often imagined to be androgynous.

The face of the moon in my picture, together with my poetic interpreta-tion, reflects the androgynous qualities associated with the moon. It may belong either to the Great Mother or to a benevolent moon god. We might even hear the theme of the Horned God echoing in the above associations.

The prognosis of alchemy in painting 8, that the lesser *sublimatio* would be followed by a *nigredo,* is fulfilled in this picture. We watched the dove's crash-flight through the fire in the previous painting, and now the world has turned dark—very dark.

The alchemists associated the motif of crucifixion with *coagulatio,* because it represents a "being nailed to matter," a being "fixated to mother earth," which was a painfully acute experience for Jürg in the ICU (Edinger 1985, p. 105). The agent for *coagulatio* is lead, a heavy and dull metal con-nected to the planet Saturn with its astrological qualities of depression, mel-ancholy, and galling limitation. The substance to be coagulated is the elusive quicksilver, the spirit Mercurius. It signifies that Mercurius, whom Edinger describes as "the autonomous spirit of the archetypal psyche, the paradoxi-cal manifestation of the transpersonal Self" must be connected with "heavy reality and the limitations of personal particularity" (ibid., pp. 85–86). The alchemists' conception of the darkest *nigredo* included *mortificatio* and *putre-factio*—the suffering and rotting in one's misery, the struggle in the face of an incomprehensible fate. It is the myth of Inanna at the moment of being killed in the presence of her dark sister Ereshkigal and hung up on a peg to rot; it is the biblical Job castigated by the dark side of Yahweh; it is Dante's *Inferno.* This painting and poem, in particular, are a testimony of how the reality of the brain tumor and its present and future consequences severely tested the limitations of our personal particularities. Experiences of satori and enlighten-ment were being challenged; the pursuit of a glamorous career as a transplant surgeon was suddenly thwarted by what we experienced as an ugly blow of fate. The very core of our substance was being tested, and only what was real had the power to get us through.

To the moon, Luna, the alchemists attributed a coagulating effect. Jacob Boehme writes that "the other [planetary] forms do all cast their desire through Sol into Luna; for in Sol they are spiritual and in Luna corporeal" (quoted in Edinger 1985, p. 96). From this perspective, the moon then empha-sizes the theme of *coagulatio* with its morbid imagery. But the face in my painting is a complex image: although the sickle of a waning moon frames it (a sickle like the personification of death as skeletal man so often carries in his hand), the actual face is that of a full moon with a benevolent expression. It contains a promise: "The clear moonlight of the *albedo* leads the adept out of the black night of the soul (the *nigredo*)" (Abraham 1998, p. 5).

Painting 11

I had probably started out with one diagonal fold, but then let myself be possessed for a moment with anger and frustration, which translated into crumpling the paper in my fist. The gesture is symbolic of a centering and gathering of energies, as in the German expression *sich zusammen nehmen*, in the sense of getting one's act together. Visually, the manipulation gives the painting the appearance of batik; psychologically, it may suggest complexity; poetically, it became a metaphor for the puzzle of the world. The new face appears from within a dark cloud (its one slanted eye a suggestion in the dried paint), while the blue and yellow colors around the margins give the impression of sunshine and blue sky. It came as a complete surprise after the dark mood of the previous picture. The poem states, "I am back," but, as in most of my poems, it is ambiguous, leaving open to whom this new face belongs. Understandably, the wish that Jürg as my hero would be back, restored to his full human capacity, was burning in my soul. I remember vividly, and it elicits a rueful smile even now, how the white patches surrounding the face reminded me of the headdress of a Bedouin, which immediately made me think of Lawrence of Arabia (as portrayed in the movie with the same title). Yet I was fully cognizant that Jürg was far from it: the German *noch nicht auf die Beine gestellt*, ("not yet being on [his] feet") may literally refer to Jürg, who was making shaky efforts to walk again. Conversely, the expression *noch fehlen Hand und Fuss* ("not having hands and feet"—a German colloquialism meaning that something does not yet have a tangible reality) may be a metaphor alluding to the new perspective awakening within myself, which was not yet put into practice, not yet tested by reality. In that sense, I found myself mirrored as well. In the act of painting and crumpling the paper, I had resurfaced from the terribly depressive state with a new perspective.

The face was all I had focused on at the time, and only with reference to my husband. But how surprised I was when revisiting the paintings with new eyes to discover suddenly a full-bodied woman—nay, an awesome goddess figure! She stands naked, with a black cape or mantle covering her shoulders. Her right breast is well defined and round; her left one is dark, hanging low and off to the side. She has a round belly and round thighs—her figure altogether reminiscent of the Venus of Willendorf. On top of her white head-dress sits a dark heart turned upside down. Behind it, the shape of a crown is visible in the form of petals or a fleur-de-lis—also an emblem of the goddess.

The image impresses me as a composite of "light" and "dark" aspects. The figure is surrounded by blue and gold. The blue represents the light, spiri-tualized feminine (as discussed in the third painting), the one of the Christian Mary and the biblical Sophia. Yet she emerges out of the dark smoke column in the center—truly emerging from the dark night of the soul. In that context, her white headdress is reminiscent of the white dove, as if it were draped around her face. The dark purple, upside-down heart suggests the heart of the goddess of the underworld or of the goddess who has been through the underworld. The crown surrounding her head shimmers in gray, the combina-tion of black and white. Her face is friendly, lightly smiling, yet has an intense determination. Unlike the Venus of Willendorf, she looks directly at us. The little exercise in which one covers one side of the face and then the other yields two very different expressions, as if this goddess was a composite of the mythic Inanna and Ereshkigal: her right half is youthful, open, and direct, whereas her left half looks older, sly, and guarded. Sylvia Brinton Perera describes the qualities of these two sisters, extracted from the Sumerian poem. Inanna is "the quintessential positive puella, an eternally youthful, dynamic, fierce, sensuous harlot-virgin" (1981, p. 18). Ereshkigal represents "primal affect"; her image "shows the earlier, paradoxical potency in raw form, . . . in her power and terror, . . . and her intimate connection to nonbeing and to fate" (ibid., p. 23).

Both with reference to myself and as a representation of Jürg's anima, it would hint at the dark side of the archetypal feminine, with the potential of raw, more primal (and, in Jürg's case, hard to control) affects coming to the fore, and we know from the story that this was indeed so. Integrating these forces would take years of concentrated psychological work. From today's perspective, it seems to me, this new face in my painting is beautifully sym-bolic of an attitude that is able to hold the tension of the opposites between the light and the dark aspects of the feminine.

Alchemically, the white headdress of the goddess figure may point to the *albedo*, the promise of the full moon in the previous picture. As Marlan, like Hillman, reminds us, color symbolism in alchemy points to momentary psychic states and "changes in coloration reflect subtle changes in the soul" (2005, p. 188). However, reading established color sequences as linear, progressive, and irreversible, with a "literal salvational goal" in mind, does justice neither to alchemical wisdom nor to real life (ibid.). Most importantly, the *nigredo,* the blackness, is never left behind completely; it becomes a part of the perspective, as reflected, I would think, in the myth of Inanna: the goddess is said to have come back to the upper world from her descent with "the eye of death" (see, for example, Perera 1981, pp. 30–34 and 78).

Woodman and Dickson, who in their book reclaim the presence of the goddess in our lives, write about her as divine immanence. The authors compare the quality of this energy with "recent scientific discoveries concerning the 'light in matter,'" referring to nonlinear theories in new physics, such as chaos theory (1969, p. 5). For alchemy (the "old science"), the light in matter, the *lumen naturae,* represented a most meaningful notion as well. Such was the foremost preoccupation of the medieval Swiss physician and alchemist Paracelsus, who contended that the heavenly light from above would make the darkness still darker, "but the *lumen naturae* is the light of the darkness itself, which illuminates its own darkness, and this light the darkness comprehends" (quoted in Jung 1942, par. 197). Jung comments:

> Paracelsus, like all philosophical alchemists, was seeking for something that would give him a hold on the dark, body-bound nature of man, on the soul which, intangibly interwoven with the world and with matter, appeared before itself in the terrifying form of strange, demoniacal figures and seemed to be the secret source of life-shortening diseases. (Ibid., par. 198)

Still today, with all our medical innovations, illness can remind us with terrifying imagery of our body-bound and death-bound nature. But the alchemists' insight was, as Jung puts it, that "nature not only contains a process of transformation—it is itself transformation" (ibid.). This was the light in nature, which the alchemists personified as feminine figures (akin to Jung's notion of the anima) with whom they aspired to enter into a union, a "chymical wedding"— in Jung's words, "a well-nigh eschatological experience" (ibid., par. 225). We don't know how Maria Prophetissa would have experienced and written about this phenomenon. For a woman, it has more to do with the recognition of being mirrored in the selfhood, of sameness and belonging. The experience of the goddess's divine essence is akin to the experience of the numinous Self— it, too, is of eschatological proportions.

Painting 12

Continuing my play with the artistic technique, I applied the paint differently here, in a patchier manner, leaving much empty space in between. Although I folded the paper, hardly any folds are visible. It gives this painting a quite different aesthetic appeal from what we have seen so far.

The center and left portion of the picture is occupied by the three animals: deer, fox, and dove. The light brown deer is sitting in the shaded area in the center. Its one visible eye is displaced, located farther back in the throat area where I had discovered the shape in the dried paint and faithfully rendered it. The deer, perhaps a doe, looks cute and innocent, but its eye is staring with a frightened expression into the lower right area. The red fox comes in from the left side and looms large next to the doe. In contrast to the doe's, its one eye is luminous and reflective, seeming to look out into far-off horizons. Both animals are poised as though they are expecting something to happen. The most striking object, however, is the white dove, limp and lifeless, imprisoned in a container that looks like a black bomb.

The picture has an eerie, otherworldly, and sinister quality, which the poem captures succinctly: "A storm is brewing / Heavy rain is coming down / And missiles are flying through the air." Indeed, the patchy paint on the right side of the picture renders the impression of elements being stirred up. The image and the poem metaphorically express the prevailing mood and real-life circumstances. Jürg's homecoming, his unstable emotional disposition, and his unexpected hostile demeanor toward me had created worries and tension in myself and between the family members. How were things going to turn out?

Surprisingly, I referred to the fox and the doe as "the old, inimical brothers," thus refraining from easy attribution of the animals' meanings to persons. The poem shows that the phrase was not simply chosen for rhyme's sake and therefore must have a psychological significance. Taken as inner psychic dynamics, research into the symbolism of fox and deer brings some interesting insights. The most significant aspect of the deer is its connection with the otherworld as a "conductor of souls," representing "non-ordinary awareness or the capacity to communicate with the spirit world" (Chevalier and Gheerbrant 1969, p. 282; Henderson and Sherwood 2003, p. 43). In Irish mythology, the goddess "as a Primeval Mother . . . is known as a supernatural deer" (Gimbutas 1989, p. 319). For the Celts, deer are "the supernatural animals of the fairy world and are fairy cattle and divine messengers" (Cooper 1978, p. 50). The deer was frequently associated with the tree of life and was sacred to the Egyptian goddess Isis and to the Greek goddesses Artemis, Athena, and Aphrodite, also often depicted as resting beside the Virgin Mary.

Sams and Carson's *Medicine Cards: The Discovery of Power through the Ways of Animals,* which is based on Native American lore, praise the gentleness of the deer. The legend of how Fawn, on its way to the Great Spirit on Sacred Mountain, overcame the demonic monster simply with love and gentleness serves as a reminder "to find the gentleness of spirit that heals all wounds" and to "stop pushing so hard to get others to change, and love them as they are" (1988, p. 54).

The fox, on the other hand, is well known in Europe as a sly and cunning trickster figure. Because of its reddish fur, the animal is associated with fire and therefore counts "among the devil's followers" (Becker 1992, p. 143). In that capacity, the animal partakes in the ancient goddess symbolism. In ancient Rome the fox was a "fire demon," used in ritual at the feast of the goddess Ceres: cruelly, "foxes were chased through the fields with burning torches on their tails to ward off grain fires" (Biedermann 1989, p. 143).

But the Native American lore emphasizes the fox's positive qualities: "Fox medicine involves adaptability, cunning, observation, integration, and swiftness of thought and action," as well as decisiveness and "sure-footedness in the physical world" (Sams and Carson 1988, p. 137). The most significant association for my situation at the time, it seems to me, is the fox's character as the protector of the family unit. The Great Spirit "honors Fox with the duty of keeping the family together and safe. This is accomplished through Fox's ability to observe undetected, without making others self-conscious" (ibid.). In this view, the fox, as the one who makes the connection with the physical world, symbolizes the extravert counterpart to the introverted deer.

These two "brothers" thus represented a polarity within my psyche, which I grasped without awareness of their deeper meaning: one makes the connection to the dimensions of spirit; the other is sure-footed in the physical world. They had been held together under the demands of a strenuous life within the bond of marriage, in which husband and wife participated as a team. In my perception at the time, they were in danger of turning against each other during the crisis with its upheaval and confusion. Traditionally, the duty to keep the family together and safe is a role assigned to the father. Perhaps I intuited the suggestion contained in the image that a role reversal was about to take place. Wilber (2000), in his moving account of his wife's struggle with breast cancer and how he coped with it, writes about his realization that he had to learn to become a wife, admitting that it was a difficult adjustment. Similarly, my task ahead was going to be an equally difficult role reversal, because I would have to learn to become a husband and take over the duty of keeping the family together in a more sovereign and assertive way than I had so far. As suggested by the symbolic associations of the imagery, it was a matter of tending to both the extraverted and the introverted facets of my existence and of holding them together in a more conscious way.

The image of the dove in the black container situated between the two "inimical brothers" pertains to the same cluster of symbolic associations. In this context, it most obviously represents peace, wrapped in an instrument of war, a bomb that could go off at any moment. On a deeper level, however, it harks back to the dove in painting 9, which I connected with Inanna's descent to her underworldly sister, Ereshkigal. Here, the dove is in a dangerously volatile situation, and the outcome is uncertain.

Where alchemy is concerned, Jung writes that the white dove is "another symbol of Mercurius, who, in his volatile form of *spiritus*, is a parallel of the Holy Ghost" (1952b, par. 518). Jung quotes the alchemist Johannes Grasseus who describes the *prima materia* as lead that "contains the radiant white dove . . . called the 'salt of the metals'" within it (1955–56, par. 443). In the alchemist's vivid imagination, "this is the chaste, wise, and rich Queen of Sheba, veiled in white, who was willing to give herself to none but King Solomon. No human heart can sufficiently investigate all this" (ibid., par. 533). I wholeheartedly agree. Grasseus then offers the analogy between the queen of Sheba and Mercurius (as dove), for "he, too, has left his own lands and clothed himself with the fairest garment of white" (ibid.).

The queen of Sheba! Perhaps she was veiled in white, but there was a dark mystery about her. In Rivkah Schärf-Kluger's (1995) charming essay, the queen emerges from the old Jewish, Arabic, and Christian legends as an immensely complex ("rich") and mysterious figure. The legends revolve around her visit to King Solomon and their mutual attraction. Having heard about his knowledge and wisdom, she had accepted his invitation in the hope of finding a cure for her ailment. He, in turn, had heard rumors from the djinns that she was a demon, and he was curious about this queen of the south who was said to rule over the garden of Eden. He devised an ingenious ruse to test her, and so "he saw that she had hairy legs" (Schärf-Kluger 1995, p. 79). In an Arabic version, she even had the feet of an ass—this was the ailment for which she sought a cure.

Schärf-Kluger points out that this nonhuman stigma relates the queen to the demonic Lilith, Adam's first wife, who roamed with "the hairy ones" in the desert (ibid., p. 80). According to her, the meeting and union of the queen of Sheba with King Solomon is a story of redemption. From a Jungian perspective, she writes that the legends portray the inner drama "not so much as a development of the anima, but as a development of the woman who submits to a higher animus form" (ibid., p. 85). The queen of Sheba, an Amazon-like virgin queen on her journey to find healing, is an image symbolic of "displaced, or unredeemed masculinity" in women, seeking and finding redemption (ibid., p. 84). In alchemical terms, the union represents a *coniunctio*, which, as Schärf-Kluger points out, found its most complete expression in connection with the redemption of the dark queen, because "it still embraces darkness and light . . . . The queen of Sheba is the Virgin Earth, the feminine Mercury [as dove], and, as queen, the heaven in which the sun shines" (ibid., p. 99). The metaphor Grasseus had in mind, however, might rest on another tradition, aligned with the patristic literature. In the hermeneutics of the church fathers, the *regina austri*, queen of the South, is the south wind, hot and dry, which becomes a symbol of the Holy Spirit. As Sophia-Sapientia, she is a feminine pneuma and appears personified as a figure made entirely of light (a prefiguration of Mary).

Grasseus's metaphor of the *prima materia*—lead that contains the radiant white dove—for which my painting proves to be such an apt image, holds the as yet unfulfilled potential of an inner psychic union of opposites. By the very act of painting, though, my awareness of what had been up to this point a displaced masculinity (onto the husband) and the perceived (terrifying) task of redeeming it by assuming the role of head of household was dawning on me.

Painting 13

A simple crosswise fold yielded a richly textured palette of panels saturated in green, gold, black, and red. Some patterns in the dried paint and, foremost, the two little eyes staring out of it provided the incentive to outline the crab and the beetle within it, adding the many legs, the feelers, the "tail" of the crab, and the head of the beetle with antlers (also suggested in the paint). While not biologically correct, they are close enough to be recognized for what they are.

Having dealt with the abundant cockroaches in New York City apartments, I had not been especially fond of beetles, but this one, born in my imagination, I held very special. Again, the beetle has masculine gender in German, which made it naturally a "he." I still have a felt sense today of the numinosity this little stag beetle instilled in me as I let it emerge from the dried paint. What I said about him in the poem is reminiscent of the little prince in painting 7: a secrecy surrounds him, a mystery, and he is of uncertain origin. In the case of the beetle, the poem asks whether he has grown in the belly of the crab or whether the crab has swallowed him up. Either way, like the prince, this little beetle is at home in the elemental world. Moreover, the poem says that he chooses not to show his antlers; in fact, no one even knows he has them. Perhaps no one else would be able to see what I saw — neither then nor now — because the beetle's inconspicuous horns do not qualify as "gorgeous," and no one would have even guessed that this was supposed to be a stag beetle. I was like a mother in love with her child, nurturing warm feelings toward it and perceiving a godlike and god-given beauty that only she can see. This tiny beetle-child, then, partakes with the little prince in the numinous child archetype.

There is no distinction in the German language between crab and cancer; the animal, the astrological sign, and the illness all go by the same word (*Krebs*). In my poem, there is a playful, if sad, intermingling of these meanings and their associated symbolism.

Jung states that the crab "is not a personal experience, it is an archetype" (1935, par. 90). The astrological sign of Cancer is a watery and feminine sign that is ruled by the moon. It evokes the image of the ancient moon goddess and the archetypal Great Mother. In the natural chart, Cancer occupies the house positioned in the *immum coeli*, the deepest or innermost place, associated with one's mother or father and ancestors. The sign hosts the summer solstice, after which the sun begins to retreat (like the crab's movements) and the days grow shorter. The particular movement of the crab going sideways and backward has made it an unlucky animal in superstition (in colloquial German, "to crab backward" means to retreat, or regress; in English, a "crabby" person is ill-tempered).

The Greek physician Hippocrates first named malignant tumors *carcinos (karkinos)*, meaning "crab," because the unrelenting and persistent pain seemed similar to that inflicted by the claws of a crab. Another source for the term Hippocrates coined points to the astronomical constellation Cancer, which the ancient Babylonian astrologers called "the Wicked One." In ancient Greece, it was associated with the myth of the Hydra. These images evoke the elemental Great Mother as a menacing, devouring monster, mythically represented as "'the crab woman' with two immense claws" (Neumann 1955, p. 177).

The question in my poem, as to whether the stag beetle has grown in the crab or been swallowed up, is intriguing because each possibility suggests a different story. If swallowed, the stag beetle in the belly would refer to Jürg, literally being swallowed up by the cancer, the illness. Incidentally, a Swiss colloquialism teasingly applies the word "stag" (Hirsch) to a male who is showing off his extraordinary prowess. Marie-Louise von Franz used the metaphor when talking about people doing things (including active imagination) "with their eyes fixed on power, on overcoming the difficulty, on being the big stag who did it" (quoted in Watkins 1984, p. 109, n1). In the case of Jürg as a patient, his well-known ability to perform as the big stag was, of course, thoroughly compromised. If, on the other hand, the stag beetle is imagined as having grown within the crab, it evokes a benign image of the Great Mother as womb or "vessel," nurturing the new growth within her protective shell (Neumann 1955, p. 4). The oblique question shows that I barely allowed myself to acknowledge that the image of the stag beetle in the crab might signify new life gestating deep down in my psyche—a new life I now recognize as the dynamic masculine principle, in the recurrent symbolic image of the Horned God. Similar to the first painting, here he appears in theriomorphic form. But at this stage in the process I recognized him (if only as something numinous and deeply important); I drew him out and entertained imaginings about him.

At present, I am admiring the photos of full-grown stag beetles (*Lucanus cervus*), an endangered species nowadays. It is a unique and very impressive beetle with its mighty antlers attached to its head (which are, in effect, its mandibles, put to good use by both males and females). Maria Fremlin (http://maria.fremlin.de/stagbeetles/index.html) serves up a collection of the many different names the stag beetle carries in mythology and folk legend, pointing to its symbolic significance. In England, for example, it goes by "billywitch" and is associated with witchcraft because stag beetles in flight look a bit like a witch on a broomstick. In Germany, one of its names is "thunder-beetle." It was considered the holy animal of the Germanic god of thunder, Donar (in Norse, the god Thor), possibly based on the observation that they live in old oaks damaged by lightning. In Moldova, it was known as "the priest's cow." The German painter Albrecht Dürer (1471–1528) associated the stag beetle with Christ and produced a famous watercolor of the insect.

The crab, in its symbolism as the archetypal feminine container wherein transformation happens, embodies special meaning for the alchemical opus. There, it has been linked with the alchemical vessel, "understood as the uterus where the 'child' is gestated" (Jung 1952b, par. 246, n125). The famous female alchemist, Maria Prophetissa, referred to the vessel as the *vas mirabile*, the marvelous vessel, and emphasized that the whole secret would lie in knowing it. In Henderson and Sherwood's interpretation, the vas or alembic represents "a conscious, purposeful, contained activity" (2003, p. 110), that is, contained in a protected place or *temenos*—precisely what the meditative, "alchemical" paintings were for me. The crab in my painting, then, is a fitting image for my motherly, nurturing attitude toward my own process and toward what wanted to grow in my psyche.

In alchemy, the "child" that grows within the alembic is the *filius philosophorum* (the philosophical son), none other than the spirit Mercurius in his most accomplished form. Given the stag beetle's many different names that reflect both masculine and feminine attributions, he is indeed a valid representation for the androgynous Mercurius. One of the best-known epithets for Mercurius is the fugitive stag: "In his role as the fleeing hart [stag] Mercurius serves as the messenger or soul which mediates between the spirit and the body, uniting them in the chemical wedding" (Abraham 1998, p. 32). Yet the alchemical Mercurius is ever ambivalent—either *servus* (servant) or *cervus* (stag). "In one aspect, he is a faithful ministering servant, while in the other he is volatile, elusive and evasive, even unfaithful and deceptive" (ibid., p. 33). The alchemists repeatedly warned that the unstable Mercurius must be captured and sealed tightly in the vessel. It is very well, then, that the stag beetle in my picture (who could easily fly off) is securely enclosed within the crab until he is fully grown.

The coloring, if viewed from left to right, proceeds from green to yellow to red. According to Henderson and Sherwood, the *Aurora consurgens* makes "an association between this yellow-red transition and the dawn: 'The dawn [aurora] is midway between night and day, shining with twofold hues, namely red and yellow'" (2003, p. 146). They quote Marie-Louise von Franz, who commented:

> Psychologically, this "aurora" symbol denotes a state in which there
> is a growing awareness of the luminosity of the unconscious. It is
> not a concentrated light like the sun, but rather a diffused glow on
> the horizon, [that is] on the threshold of consciousness. (Ibid., p. 146)

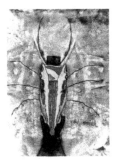

Painting 14

When holding painting 13 and 14 next to each other, no words are necessary, neither the narrative nor the poem, to understand what has happened in the time between the two—quite simply, a miracle: the stag beetle is born.

The richly textured background, with a barely visible central fold, contains many suggestive shapes and interesting patterns—eyes, snouts, or beaks of grotesque masks. Within this environment, the stag beetle emerges victorious. He comes out of a black form that looks like the tail fin of a large black whale, about to dive back into the depths of the ocean.

This stag beetle is a fantasy beetle, far more colorful than the real stag beetle in nature, or most beetles for that matter. Its body rather resembles the kind of fish that populate a coral reef, as if a colorful fish skin had been pulled over its body. I can't help but wonder what this fish skin might add to the significance of the stag beetle, and so I indulge in an exploration of fish symbolism.

To my ever-present wonderment, the symbolism of the fish reaches far back into very early prehistoric times, like that of the moon, the cross, and the egg. Thanks to her archaeological excavations, Gimbutas is able to present us with artifacts from the Upper Paleolithic, attesting to the worship of the fish goddess (recall the abyssal fish goddess at Delphi mentioned in the commentary to painting 5). Gimbutas regards the fish "a symbol of becoming"; its moistness is associated with the life-renewing moistness of the uterus (1989, p. 259). The fish, like the deer, symbolized the life-giving aspect of the goddess. A beautiful example is a Boeotian terra-cotta amphora that has been found in a tomb (ibid., fig. 405; see also Neumann [1955, plate 134], who, in this instance, refers to the goddess as "lady of the beasts"). On one panel, the goddess is shown in human form with a heart-shaped face. A stylized fish, standing on its tail, makes up the fullness of her skirt. Another panel depicts the goddess as bird with the scaled body of a fish. In both pictures, she is surrounded by animals as well as many of the graphic insignia for the goddess.

According to Jung, the astrological sign of Pisces (two fish, swimming in opposite directions) reflects the development in history of the ancient Great Mother in her representation as fish:

> Babylonian and Indian astrology know of only one fish. Later, this mother evidently gave birth to a son, who was a fish like her. The same thing happened to the Phoenician Deceto-Atargatis, who, half fish herself, had a son called Ichthys. (1951, par. 173)

However, as Jung remarks, "the mythological Great Mothers are usually a danger to their sons" (ibid., par. 174). In her representation as a fish (like the crab), the goddess's devouring aspect became predominant. For example, Adam's first demon-wife Lilith was said to have changed into a nightmare or lamia. Jung notes: "Lamia is also the name of a large, voracious fish . . . . Once again we meet the idea of the Terrible Mother in the form of a voracious fish, a personification of death" (1952c, par. 369). Walker gives us the following examples: "As the swallower of Shiva's penis, Kali became Minaksi the 'fish-eyed' one, just as in Egypt, Isis, the swallower of Osiris's penis, was known as Abtu, 'the Great Fish of the Abyss'" (1983, p. 314). The biblical story of Jonah who was swallowed by the whale comes to mind as well, an example of the "heroic night sea journey and conquest of death, where the hero is swallowed up by a fish ('whale-dragon') and is then reborn" (Jung 1951, par. 173).

120

In Christianity, writes Jung, "Christ was assimilated into a world of ideas that seems far removed from the gospels—a world of pagan origin, saturated with astrological beliefs to an extent that we can scarcely imagine today (1951, par. 172). Christ's acronym in Greek was *ichthys*, "fish," in which the individual letters spell out "Jesus Christ, Son of God, Savior." Walker notes that Christ's acronym *ichthys* was also symbolized by the lozenge, "the same way as the goddess's yoni, by two crescent moons [in Gimbutas's view, two pubic triangles] forming a *vesica piscis*," or "vessel of the fish" (1983, p. 313). Walker continues:

> In biblical terms, "Jesus son of Maria" meant the same as Yeshua son of Marah, or Joshua son of Nun (Exodus 33:11), which also means son of the Fish-mother. Mary's many Mesopotamian names like Mari, Marriti, Nar-Marratu, Mara, were written like the Hebrew Mem with an ideogram meaning both "sea" and "mother." The next letter in the Hebrew sacred alphabet was Nun, "fish." (Ibid., p. 314)

It is uncanny how the imagery in my two paintings reflect these ancient mythological themes. The crab as a representation of the Great Mother could be either the voracious monster that has swallowed the stag beetle, her "son," or an image of the "creatrix," as Gimbutas has it, who gestated him in her womb (1989, p. xxii). Whether grown or reborn, here he emerges victorious from what looks like the tail end of the mythic black sea monster or, indeed, like Jonah from the whale. He is a stag beetle, yet with his fish-skin coat, he is "like his mother." From a psychological perspective, as stated above, he truly embodied for me the dynamic animus, who animated me and motivated me, as the saying goes, to come out of my shell and show my colors.

Within the alchemical opus, the stag beetle's coat not only has significance in its association with the fish. The blue and yellow (gold) colors it displays have meaning in themselves. These colors have appeared before, in paintings 3 and 11. There, they are part of the initial chaos and blend in with the environment, infusing the figures or the background. Here, I had dressed the central figure in blue and yellow with the same deliberation with which I had put the yellow-golden crown on the little prince's head.

According to Elkins, yellow and blue as a pair represent one of the many synonyms for "the founding alchemical pair of sulfur and mercury" (2000, p. 53). Abraham notes that sulphur is the "hot, dry, active seed of metals, the male principle, Sol, in the opus alchymicum" (1998, p. 193). Mercury, or *argent vive*, is the feminine principle, Luna, "the cold, moist, receptive, female seed of metals" (ibid., p. 10). However, these are not simply the metals as they come from the earth. It is philosophical sulfur, "an abstract principle, an inherent constitutive element within matter. . . . [It] constitutes the 'form' of the metal" (ibid., p. 193). The philosophical mercury, on the other hand, is equated with the "matter" of the metal. Sulphur has the power to fix and coagulate the volatile spirit, whereas *argent vive,* or Mercury, has the power to dissolve fixed matter. These two elements or principles must be united in the alchemical wedding in order to conceive the philosophical stone, the *lapis philosophorum* (which goes under so many names, including *infans, puer, filius philosopho-rum, Hermaphroditus*), representing, in Jung's words, "the polarity and union of opposites, which is just what gives the *lapis philosophorum* its peculiar significance as a uniting symbol and hence its magical and divine properties" (1951, par. 216). Jung refers to some very early alchemical texts that denote the fish as a "symbol for the arcane substance and the *lapis*" (ibid., par. 194). Moreover, the alchemist Ripley contends that fishes "appear in their 'messi-anic' role: together with the birds, they bring the stone" (quoted in Jung 1951, par. 224). It is, Jung reminds us, the motif of the helpful animal, just as in the Oxyrhynchus sayings of Jesus: "It is the 'fowls of the air and the fishes of the sea and whatsoever is upon or beneath the earth' that point the way to the kingdom of heaven" (ibid., par. 224).

None of this was known to me at the time, but by painting the stag beetle the way I did, I gave image to what was stirring in my psyche, and I could certainly feel the stag beetle's numinous energy intensely.

Painting 15

I had been turning to my meditation daily since it started, but between the last painting and this one almost a week had passed. Even without the narrative, we would be moved to assume that a dark and painful mood must have been the incentive for this painting. It marks such a drastic shift, an *enantiodromia*, from the image of the glorious stag beetle to the pitch-black blob in the middle of the gold displayed here. The narrative tells us about the dispute between myself and my husband and the rupture in our relationship. The dreaded storm I had anticipated in painting 12 had come about after all.

I now wonder whether the irrational spark of rebellion with which I had resisted my husband's intent hadn't been the influence of the stag beetle's glorious appearance. Indeed, seen from a Jungian perspective, the numinous, dynamic animus figure, which had given me the impulse to share my art-work, evidently also must have inflated me to some degree. The stag beetle, being a theriomorphic symbol, had infused me with instinctual archetypal energy, which I could not so suddenly integrate into ego consciousness (see Jung1952c, par. 505). Edinger (1972) mentions inflation precisely within the context of the daimonic, ecstatic, and wild Dionysian energy (of which, admit-tedly, I had gotten only a small dose, but it was enough to create a scene). Edinger's clinical experience shows that a state of inflation by Dionysian energy most often turns into its opposite, a deflation, and this is what I expressed in my painting with the choice of colors: a black blob, squeezing out the golden yellow. I felt devastated and depressed to the degree of not giving this painting a chance to allow a connection with the deep psyche—not even after all the marvelous moments I had witnessed in the process so far.

For the second time, I had rendered an image of the dark night of the soul, but there is a substantial difference between the two. The first one, "Golgotha" (painting 10) was more a reflection of the misery brought about by Jürg's illness, accompanied by dark thoughts about human existence. With this one, I was sitting in honest consternation about my own dark side, my shadow; while staring into the black that spread over the golden yellow, I looked into a black hole. In this moment of complete surrender I received the soul's ministration most powerfully, as it was a profound revelation to recognize the smiling face in the darkness. Unlike the Golgotha painting, this one contained a redemptive quality. It made me acknowledge the divine wisdom of the soul that revealed itself precisely in the deepest darkness. And I accepted the gift as it was; I didn't feel the need to add anything with brush and paint.

With the immersion into Zen Buddhism over many years, I naturally interpreted the features I perceived as the smiling face of the Buddha. Now, as with painting 7, I see a feminine face—the smiling face of the Black Madonna, perhaps, or of Kwan Yin, the Chinese goddess of compassion. Either way, it is a divine face. The u-shaped oval that surrounds the features is gently outlined. The eyes rest deeply in the shadow, overarched by eyebrows that seem pulled together in a frown. But the mouth is highlighted and is sweetly smiling. I also see two pairs of vocal chords, one located right under the chin in the black, the other farther down in the golden neck. A most portent message, then as now, it suggests that, infused with divine love, I can speak my truth from the light and from the dark side.

I still hold the figure sitting at the location of the third eye to be a Buddha figure or perhaps that of a Tibetan monk, sitting in lotus position. He wears a white robe and an extravagant headdress that rises and fans out from a small black band sitting on top of his head. Psychologically, he represents the highest form of animus, an enlightened perspective. The image is an illustration, it seems to me, of the promise contained in our efforts at reviving the dark aspects of the goddess. It is not a regression to ancient matriarchal times, where she may have wielded her raw force unreflectively. Rather, the image suggests that, as her dark power is embodied in women today, it may be guided by insight, wisdom, and consciousness.

Alchemically speaking, I think this paint blot represents a prime image of the *sol niger*, the black sun. Round and dark, it eclipses the golden light, still visible around the edges. If the sun, *sol*, represents the Self, then *sol niger* is its shadow, its negation, its deconstruction; it stands for the no-self or non-self.[15] *Sol niger* is associated with the *nigredo*, *mortificatio*, and *putrefactio*, that is, with extreme suffering and depression; it is an imaginal expression of annihilation. These themes of depression and despair were perhaps closer to physical death and more dramatically represented in painting 10; there, they were a momentary reflection of Jürg's dire condition in the hospital. This painting, on the other hand, refers to psychological suffering, implying the subtle body and the potential for its transformation. It remains, then and now, a very moving image of the *lumen naturae*, "the light of darkness itself, which illuminates its own darkness, and this light the darkness comprehends" (Jung 1942, par. 197). In other words, it is not just a black hole that sucks all the light and energy into itself. It is alive and enlivening with its own imagery; it is numinous and mythopoeic, so much so that, at the time, I was awestruck and didn't have any of my own words to express my experience, except to stammer "res sacra miser."

There is meaning within the sequence of imagery between the previous painting and this one. Given the developments in daily life, the epiphany of the stag beetle's birth clearly represented a lesser *coniunctio,* which, according to Edinger, is "a union or fusion of substances that are not yet thoroughly separated or discriminated" (1985, p. 211). Edinger is unequivocal:

> The lesser *coniunctio* occurs whenever the ego identifies with contents emerging from the unconscious . . . . The ego is exposed successively to identifications with the shadow, the anima/animus, and the Self. Such contaminated *coniunctios* must be followed by *mortificatio* and further *separatio.* (Ibid., p. 215)

124

In part (perhaps for lack of guidance and the interpretation that might have been afforded by formal analysis), the *mortificatio* and the *separatio* were acted out in reality, as we, the couple, were physically and emotionally separated after the hurtful dispute. This painting marks the return to the inner work that helped me accept the bitter truth of my own darkness. The alchemists considered it essential to return to the stage of *nigredo*, to chaos (which, psychologically, is better understood as a deliberately introverted act, not an unconscious acting out, as happened in my case before I turned inward). Jung notes that the alchemists regarded the *prima materia* (chaos) to be "corrupt and bitter" (1955–56, par. 245). The quality of *amaritudo,* bitterness, was linked with salt and the sea. Jung quotes from the *Liber Alze*: "O nature of this wondrous thing, which transforms the body into spirit! . . . When it is found alone it conquers all things, and is an excellent, harsh, and bitter acid, which transmutes gold into pure spirit" (ibid.). Salt, therefore, as Jung points out, contains both bitterness and wisdom:

Tears, sorrow, and disappointment are bitter, but wisdom is the comforter in all psychic suffering. Indeed, bitterness and wisdom form a pair of alternatives; where there is bitterness wisdom is lacking, and where wisdom is there can be no bitterness. (Ibid., par. 330)

With this particular painting, I experienced the transmutation from one into the other. By smearing black color onto the paper, I created an image of the black *prima materia* as an expression of bitterness. After folding it (*separatio*) and opening it up again, the dried paint (*coagulatio*) revealed an image that conveyed wisdom. The moment I recognized it, my bitterness vanished, and I was deeply moved by the gift I felt I had received.

Jung points out that the alchemists imagined salt as "the bird of Hermes . . . because salt is a spirit, a volatile substance" (1955–56, par. 246). We have met this bird last in painting 12, in the image of the dove trapped in the black container. The dove was described as the salt in the metal and compared with the queen of Sheba. In this painting of momentous transformation, the bird appears in a new guise too: it now sits, in the form of the Buddhist monk with his feathery headdress, in the location of the third eye, the eye of wisdom.

Here, the salt has been extracted. In alchemy, moreover, this bird is said to undergo a process of changing colors: "At first the bird is black, then it grows white feathers, which finally become coloured" (ibid., par. 248). Jung, therefore, interprets salt as Eros (that is, as a feeling relationship); confirmation "is found in the fact that the bitterness is the origin of the *colours*" and, empirically, "colours are feeling-values" (ibid., par. 333). This observation realizes itself in my process as well: the next painting will explode with color.

Painting 16

There is an intermission of almost two weeks between the last painting and this one, while I found myself engaged in the outer world. On the deepest inner psychic level, however, from where the dark Buddha/Madonna had originated, a period of incubation might well have been a felt need. Looking back, I can only imagine that the dark smiling face was a steady companion through those difficult and demanding two weeks. Unfortunately, with the dream journals of that period lost and my memory vague, I don't remember whether at any point during that time I showed the painting to my husband. If I did, it would have aided in our attempts at reconciliation, for I do know that he would have appreciated it.

Finally, there comes this painting, coinciding with and influenced by the arrival of my sister-in-law. It turns out to be the most vibrantly colorful of the series, radiating vitality and apparent joie de vivre.

Various elements from former paintings are reiterated in this picture, pregnant here with new meaning—most conspicuously the glowing red globe in the center. Whereas in painting 1 it was about to sink into the ocean, into temporary dissolution and transformation in the underworld, it now has come up from the depths again, more beautiful than before. Moreover, rather than floating on the water, the red globe is now gracefully held in a purple chalice with a long stem and a secure footing. In my imagination, the red globe is feeding a candle, burning with a small, flickering flame. The image of the horse has returned as well. In comparison to the haggard and wretched horses flanking the little prince in painting 7, this one looks well fed and in its full power. Nestled within the horse sits a green hen, the outline of her body imitating the curves of the horse's round belly. The hen, in turn, wraps around the red chalice like a feathery ornament.

Quite in contrast to the intense joy and exuberance emanating from the painting, the mood of my poem is cautious and subdued: there wasn't supposed to be an openly roaring fire; the red globe may feed only a little candle, and the hen is brooding "to avert misfortune." I believe these poetic lines express the wisdom gained over the past few weeks: rather than being too exuberant and carried away with renewed inflation, I had attempted to regulate these nascent energies more consciously. My play with the metaphor of fire reflects the transformation in progress: it moves from an openly roaring fire (the German lichterloh, as in painting 9) to candlelight, the smallest burning fire. In cultural history, the invention of the candle comes at a much later stage than the use of fire. Rather than producing heat, its practical use is to give light. The candle associates with interiority and evokes images of illuminated altars in churches and temples. The caution I expressed also has a direct reference to the status of Jürg's recovery. Seen through the eyes of my sister-in-law, I became aware just how fragile my husband still was. His emaciated body was in great need of extra care and circumspection, and his fragile nervous system was far from tolerating much excitement and turbulence.

Henderson and Sherwood's interpretation of the image of a red central

126

disk in a woman's dream to indicate "powerful libidinal forces . . . [which] now orient to a newly emerging center" could easily be a statement made with regard to the stage I had attained in my process (2003, p. 136). In that respect, the horse and hen, both theriomorphic symbols, add to the representation of vitality (powerful libidinal forces) and thus an earthy, embodied, feminine energy. The animals look female: the horse could be pregnant, and the hen is said to be brooding. The colors brown and green—the blessed greenness so emphatically praised by Hildegard of Bingen—are the colors of the earth and of vegetation (Flanagan 1989). Incidentally, Jung mentions the brooding hen as containing a "hidden fire"; the warmth of incubation, he maintains, is symbolically "equivalent to the self-incubation or the 'brooding' state of meditation," which aims at transformation and resurrection (1952b, par. 441). The horse's apparently enormous energy is similarly contained, waiting, as my poem says, for the "right moment"—*kairos* in Greek (von Franz 1997, p. 8).

Surprising to me even today, I named the horse in my painting Wotan. In reality, this is not an uncommon name for a mighty and energetic stallion or gelding. As I understand it, my *Wotanross* is emphatically a horse named Wotan and not Wotan's gray, eight-legged horse Sleipnir, which is generally less well known. In Germanic mythology, Sleipnir is the "symbol of the gallows tree" on which Odin (the Norse equivalent of Wotan) hung and bled (Walker 1983, p. 411). I doubt that I had been aware of what I quite naively conjured up by associating my horse with Wotan (horse owners in real life who do the same most likely aren't either). In his eloquent essay, Jung writes: "Wotan is the god of storm and frenzy, the unleasher of passions and the lust of battle; moreover he is a superlative magician and artist in illusion who is versed in all secrets of an occult nature" (1936, par. 375). He is a one-eyed hunter-god, a restless wanderer roving through the night. Wotan had "an ancient connection with the figures of Christ and Dionysus" (ibid., par. 373). Jung speaks of "an archetype Wotan," an autonomous and irrational psychic factor, and "a fundamental attribute of the German psyche" (ibid., pars. 391 and 389). Wotan represents "a totality on a very primitive level," who may seize (*ergreifen*) individuals and nations alike (ibid., par. 395). Here, then, by the sheer naming of the horse, I was in touch with the dynamic masculine principle again—dangerous if unconsciously autonomous but helpful if harnessed as a down-to-earth, serving and guiding animus.

Archetypally, the horse is connected to both lunar and solar symbolism. Jung describes its lunar symbolism in association with the unconscious (to which he assigned feminine gender):

Legend attributes properties to the horse which psychologically belong to the unconscious of man: there are clairvoyant and clairaudient horses, path-finding horses . . . horses with mantic powers . . . . Horses also see ghosts. All these things are typical manifestations of the unconscious. (1952c, par. 421)

Whereas the lunar symbolism is associated with the elements of earth and water, the solar symbolism connects the horse with fire, light, wind, the celestial, and with the heroic masculine: "symbol of strength, of the creative forces, and of youth," embodying "a spiritual valence" (Chevalier and Gheerbrant 1969, p. 523). Moreover, the horse's color in my painting links it with the Celtic heroic literature, where warrior horses are "often characterized by their chestnut coats, the colour of fire" (ibid., p. 525). The horse, then, embodying both lunar and solar symbolism, holds within itself a pair of opposites. In painting 12, these opposites—the magical-mystic and the valiant-heroic—were represented as a visible duality by the deer and the fox; there they were two hostile brothers. In this painting, the pair of opposites is now united and held in a single form.

More so than in the painting 1, the purple chalice holding the glowing red globe in the center evokes the image of the grail, of which Whitmont writes: "The *very centrality* of the Grail symbol has exerted a magnetic pull. Many images cluster in orbit around it" (1997, p. 153; emphasis added). Indeed, the horse and the hen in my picture visually emphasize the very centrality of the chalice by surrounding it. Whitmont considers the grail to represent the "key myth to the transformations desired in our times" (ibid., p. ix), the myth for the Aquarian age.

In the following passage, Whitmont gives an inspired description of the grail's far-reaching meanings, bringing together many of the symbols and mythologems we encountered and contemplated throughout my series of paintings:

The Grail is a wondrous vessel, a wellspring of life-giving, life-restoring waters, and a cornucopia of nourishment, a cup made of Helen's breast: it is a miraculous stone, or a man's head, or the secret primeval tradition of the mysteries. It is in the care of a goddess or a beautiful maiden. It is guarded by heroic knights in a magical castle in the land of *yonder*, in paradise, the land of the spirits, or of fairies. As an ancient cauldron, it renews life and restores youth. It is an endless source of food and sustenance, of joy, pleasure and

feasting, as well as of the ecstasies of Venus. As a vessel, it is the
cup from which Christ drank at the Last Supper. It received his blood
as it poured out of his wounds at the Crucifixion. As a stone, it is a
jewel from Lucifer's crown, brought to earth by those angels who
took no part in the conflict between God and Devil. In medieval lore,
vessel, Grail and womb, as well as *lapis* ("stone"), were still synonymous images for Mary, the mother of God.

The Grail is associated with a spear, . . . or with a king suffering
from an incurable, ever-festering wound on his genitals, or with a
stag-headed shamanic figure or magician who is kin to the Celtic
Cerunnus, the Norse Odin, or the Roman Pluto, the Greek Hades,
Dionysus, and the Chaldaic Dumuzi or Tammuz. In the latter figure,
we readily recognize the Dionysian companion of the Goddess.

Another figure associated with the Grail is a woman with boar
teeth, hair like pig's bristles, doglike nose, bear's ears, a hairy face,
and fingernails like a lion's claw. This creature of terrifying ugliness
reminds one of the Greek Medusa or the Sumerian Ereshkigal, the
dark death aspects of the Goddess or of the Sphinx. (Ibid., pp.

154–155)

For the alchemists, the grail "is closely related to the Hermetic vessel" (Jung
1952b, par. 246). Jung writes: "The stone, like the grail, is itself the creative
vessel, the *elixir vitae*" (ibid., par. 245, n124).

The red globe held by the chalice as the central image in my painting takes on an additional alchemical meaning through its placement and
because of its color. Jung notes that the accentuation of the center is a fundamental idea in alchemy. The center is actually known as "the house of fire"
(1942, par. 186). It contains the "'indivisible point,' which is simple, indestruc-
tible, and eternal" (ibid.). The alchemist Dorn said that "there is nothing more
like God than the center, for it occupies no space, and cannot be grasped,
seen, or measured. Such too is the nature of God and the spirits" (ibid.). He
calls the center "an infinite abyss of mysteries" and "the center of the natural
wisdom, whose circumference, closed in itself, forms a circle: an immeasurable order reaching to infinity" (ibid., par. 187). And, as if describing my painting, Jung comments:

Like the sun in the heavens, the balsam in the heart is a fiery, radiant
center. We meet this solar point in the Turba, where it signifies the
"germ of the egg, which is in the yolk, and that germ is set in motion
by the *hen's warmth*." (Ibid., par. 188, emphasis added)

James Hillman, in turn, reminds us that "alchemical gold is a *red* elixir . . . It is active and incarnated, a universal medicine, a multiplying power in the world, a philosopher-king" (1980, p. 26).

The reddish dawn in the background of painting 13 was the soul's premonition of the approaching completion, the *rubedo* stage, which for the alchemist "represents the final result of transformation" and "the end of the process" (Henderson and Sherwood 2003, p. 47 and p. 148, respectively). (Keeping in mind Hillman's caveat that, as long as we live, the process never really comes to an end.) Here, the intense red color of the globe contained in the crimson, purplish-red chalice announces the *rubedo* stage in its fullness. Henderson and Sherwood, quoting von Franz, offer this psychological interpretation: it "would refer to the new life that appears spontaneously after libido is freed from the complex" (ibid., p. 15). Regarded as a feminine religious symbol, it is for a woman a representation of the Self.

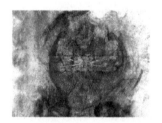

Painting 17

One cannot help but smile back at the image of this figure—woman, priestess, goddess, with a funny cat face and paws, or a cat with a woman's body—raising her arms in a gesture of joyful being-in-her-power.

In this painting, the vitality is expressed more in the gesture of the figure than in the colors. The color scheme is darker and subdued. The mystical purple moving in from the left and the blessed green coming from the right mix into an earthy conglomerate in the middle. The glowing red of the globe has transformed itself into the crimson dress of the woman as if in a natural and organic progression. The gesture of her arms still traces its round shape. She has a woman's body in a red dress and an almost-human face, only her whiskers and the green "funny hat" characterize her as a cat. Chevalier and Gheerbrant note: "To wear a special headdress is to state a difference, to distinguish a particular rank or dignity and to choose a particular path . . . . It is one of the images of the deep personality" (1969, p. 478). Indeed, I view this figure as an image of the archetypal goddess, materialized from the deep unconscious psyche. In the painting, she arises out of a diffuse darkness, similar to the goddess in painting 12. There, I did not recognize her, but now I do. With this last painting, I felt her divinity intuitively, without calling her a goddess. My studies have shown that both her embodiment as cat and her particular gesture have symbolic significance.

In ancient Egypt, the cat was sacred, perhaps her most famous representation being the great cat goddess Bastet, daughter of Isis and Osiris, who emerged in the twenty-second dynasty and took precedence over all other goddesses. Two books, Helen Luke's *The Way of Woman* (1995) and Marie-Louise von Franz's *The Cat: A Tale of Female Redemption* (1999), render a vivid portrayal, rich in mythological, psychological, and present-day significance. Von Franz describes the cat as "an extremely positive archetypal figure" (1999, p. 58). When she was identified with her father, Ra, god of life, she was a solar cat, "believed to engage every night in a struggle of cosmic proportions with Apophis, the serpent of darkness" (ibid., p. 55). In her lunar aspect, she was associated with the land of the dead and the moon, but, von Franz asserts, she had "no devilish qualities" or "witch traits" (ibid., p. 59). Luke notes that in Egypt "the name for cat means 'to see,' and Bast . . . was identified with the eyes of Horus, the sky god" (1995, p. 87). Moreover, Bastet was said to be very musical and was often depicted with a *sistrum*, the musical instrument associated with Isis. Von Franz remarks with humor, "that is because of those beautiful love songs [the cats] sing in the night, though they are not quite for our ears" (1999, p. 58).

The Illustrated Anthology of World Myth and Storytelling (Littleton 2002) depicts a famous bronze statue of Bastet (from the first millennium BCE) in her full beauty and dignity. Fitting for the celebratory mood of my last painting, the festival of Bastet attracts my attention. It was said to be one of the best-attended and most popular festivals in the Egyptian calendar. The place of the festival was Bubastis, north of Cairo, which was approached by water. A colorful description by the Greek historian Herodotus is preserved for posterity:

> They come in barges, men and women together, a great number in each boat; on the way, some of the women keep up a continual clatter with castanets and some of the men play flutes, while the rest, both men and women, sing and clap their hands. Whenever they pass a town on the riverbank, they bring the barge close inshore, some of the women continuing as I have said, while others shout abuse at the women of the place, or start dancing, or stand up and hitch their skirts. When they reach Bubastis, they celebrate the festival with elaborate sacrifices, and more wine is consumed than during all the rest of the year. (Ibid., p. 47)

What the women did, according to von Franz, was that they "lifted their skirts and showed their behinds to the applauding masses on the shore" (1999, p. 59).[16] The people paid their respects to Bastet at her red granite temple. Dead cats were taken there, Herodotus reports, "where they were embalmed and buried in sacred receptacles" and were supposed to "carry their owners' messages all the more swiftly to the realm of the gods." (Littleton 2002, p. 47). These mummified cats were discovered in underground galleries when Bastet's temple was excavated in the late 1900s.

Luke opens her essay on the archetypal cat with the question: "What does the cat mean in the psyche of man that she has acquired such a numinous quality? She inspires the most violent reactions in some people—either of attraction or repulsion—and there are not many other creatures which arouse this same kind of irrational emotion" (1995, p. 85). She substantiates her statement with personal observations that portray the cat, even when domesticated, in her nature of being one-in-herself. As an archetypal symbol the cat is ambivalent; much like the serpent, "its image oscillates between beneficence and malevolence," states von Franz (1999, p. 55). The extreme polarities are represented by the characteristics attributed to the white cat and the black cat, respectively. In its positive aspect, the cat is linked with immortality (it has nine lives); it possesses foresight and insight. The negative side of the cat is foremost associated with its eyes, which fascinate, paralyze, bewitch, and can see in the night. According to von Franz, the symbolic aspect that bridges the extreme polarity between good and evil is the cat as a medium, "with knowledge of both" (ibid., p. 57). According to a Gnostic belief, a cat guarded the tree of life with its knowledge of good and evil in the garden of Eden. Similarly, the Egyptian solar cat was associated with the tree of life and consciousness, the *Persea* tree:

> [The cat] acted as a mediator between [good and evil] as well as between interior and exterior life, god and supernatural forces and man. Because it has access to, and is at home in, both spheres, it has much prophetic wisdom to impart and can teach us how to hold conflicting values in balance. (Ibid., p. 57).

When the witch hunts began in the European Middle Ages, however, they brought a simultaneous vilification of the cat, parallel to the Church's opposing and suppressing courtly love while propagating the cult of the Virgin Mary. In fact, von Franz points out, "the black cat may be seen as the shadow side of the Virgin Mary, a projected unconscious desire for revenge against the Church" (ibid., p. 61)—the Virgin Mary herself has a cat shadow!

In von Franz's interpretation, the cat has a lot to do with the independent individuality of the feminine. She associates the cat archetype closely with "the individuation process of the feminine which cannot be forced into those conventional patterns" (ibid., p. 63). However, "as a symbol of consciousness," von Franz suggests, the cat "is a psychic entity that knows the way— *provided we learn to trust it, honoring, obeying and following wherever it leads*" (ibid., p. 57; emphasis added).

Another meaningful association to the particular posture of the cat-woman/priestess/goddess in my painting is "the goddess with upraised arms" of Egyptian and Minoan origin. Neumann views this gesture as "unquestionably religious," be it one of prayer, invocation, or magical conjuring: "The priestesses identified with the Great Mother as well as the women who worshiped her may well have assumed this same attitude." Of primary importance is the "'magical significance' of this posture . . . . And it must be remembered that the original magical intention to move and influence the upper powers is preserved in almost all prayer" (1955, ibid., pp. 114–115 and plates 26 and 27). Neumann suggests a possible second interpretation for the posture, which seems especially fitting here. It is one of epiphany, "of the moment in which the godhead appears" (ibid., p. 116).

In my process, I came to recognize *him*, the Horned God, with the birth of the stag beetle. Although I didn't know him by this name, I could feel the numinosity of the dynamic masculine principle involved and understood his importance intuitively. With this last painting, I recognized *her*, the Great Goddess. With it came the epiphany, expressed in the gesture of the raised arms, "I am woman." In the German language, *Frau* ("woman") happens to rhyme with *miau* ("meow"). Numinous and mysterious, this figure as an image of the cat goddess was naturally closer to my conscious identity as a woman than the Horned God, in whichever form, could ever be.

I did not plan for this painting to be the last one (just like the first painting had not been intended to initiate a series), but from a psychological point of view it makes sense. It appears that once the feminine and the masculine divinities have made their appearance, once they were acknowledged and paid homage to, this particular series could be concluded for the time being.

I sincerely wish I could take the image of the cat priestess/goddess to the venerable alchemist Maria Prophetissa and ask for her opinion in the matter. Consulting the literature produced by her male colleagues has not been satisfying, nor has it proven conclusive. Here is the psyche's image of the goal in my opus. She is the embodiment of femaleness and divine femininity, yet she looks very different from any of the beautiful, placid queens in the *Splendor Solis*, for example, nor quite like any other alchemical picture that is available to me. Like the ancient Egyptian goddess Bastet, she has a woman's body and the head of a cat, portraying her close connection with her instinctual nature. Although the cat has a dark side that has been vilified and diabolized, the figure in my picture is, like Bastet, an entirely positive image in her joyful assertion of life. We may assume that she consciously owns her dark side.

I have been wondering whether Maria Prophetissa might perhaps have been aware of Mercurius being portrayed as a cat (he comes in so many guises). She might gravely shake her head. Mercurius is often symbolized in theriomorphic form (we have encountered him as dove, stag, beetle; he is the swan, vulture, raven, eagle, and the mighty serpent) but never a cat. Perhaps there is a relationship between the figure in her red dress and green hat with the alchemical lion, "now green, and now red" (Jung 1948b, par. 275)? After all, lion and cat belong to the same species. But we must reject this association as well. The lion, red or green, is a "devouring predatory monster" that belongs to the beginning of the opus and is symbolically connected to the *prima materia* (Jung 1955–56, par. 404). This figure, on the other hand, is the culminating image at the end of a transformational process. Maria Prophetissa looks at me with a bemused smile at my eagerness. But I'm not ready to give up quite yet. Is Mercurius not sometimes personified in his feminine form as part theriomorphic—half animal, half woman? Indeed, as the *anima mundi*, he is Edem: "virgin above, serpent below," supposedly the origin of Paracelsus's Melusina, the mermaid (Jung 1952b, par. 413, n33). No, these images are the reverse of mine, portraying woman *as* instinctual nature and not woman *conscious of* her nature.

Comparing Mercurius in his feminine form as Luna, Eve, Regina, or queen with my cat goddess does not satisfy either. There, he or she is one half of a pair that, in *coniunctio*, makes a whole, whereas the ancient cat goddess preserves the sense of being one-in-herself. In this case "the noble whore Venus" mentioned by Kunrath and other alchemists might well qualify, as she is connected to the ancient virgin love goddess Ishtar/Astarte who is, precisely, portrayed as one-in-herself (Jung 1955–56, par. 415). However, Jung tells me that for the alchemists she "characterizes the arcane substance in its initial, 'chaotic,' maternal state," the "virgin womb of Chaos" (ibid., n182). Moreover, as Jung points out, these feminine representations, "mother, daughter, sister, bride, matron, and whore are always combined in the anima archetype," thus pertaining to the psychology of the male alchemist (ibid.).

With a deep sigh I'm ready to give up my futile searches when I see her nodding her head approvingly, even enthusiastically: but yes, yes—this *is* a worthy symbol for the goal of a woman's alchemical opus! And then she proceeds to tell me in her own language something along the lines of what

Jung intuited with his surprising remark that in a female alchemist's work the leitmotif might well have been the fiery Mars (instead of the gentle Venus), and *"not Sophia, but Hecate, Demeter, and Persephone, or the matriarchal Kali of southern India in her brighter and darker aspects"* (1946, par. 518).[17] So there we have it! I deeply appreciate Jung's acknowledgment.

Maria Prophetissa now looks at me kindly and suggests that there are plenty of alchemical associations around this image of the cat priestess/goddess. In her red dress, she pertains to the *rubedo* stage, the goal of the opus. Her green hat, the *benedicta viriditas,* indicates the potential for ongoing growth. She does share with Mercurius some very basic traits: she is duplex, of a dual nature, as she combines light and dark aspects in herself. Like Mercurius, she is of an "intermediate substance (*media substantia*)," synonymous with the concept of the soul's intermediate nature (*anima media natura*) (Jung 1948b, par. 261). Like him, she is the "ligament of the soul, uniting spirit and body" (Jung 1955–56, par. 635). However, she does not represent the initial unconscious *participation mystique* portrayed as uroboros; rather, in her form as woman with the head of a cat, she embodies a "symbol of consciousness," as von Franz says (1999, p. 57). Like Mercurius, she may be a woman's mediator in her process of individuation.

At the time I painted this picture, the image was well suited for my situation. The cat priestess/goddess, in her expression of "jest for life," did not just compensate for my looming depression and possible loss of faith in the face of a life-threatening illness. As a vital image of the archetypal divine feminine, her numinosity seems to touch every person who contemplates the picture. In Jungian psychology, she represents an archetypal image of the Self.

As Christine Downing's (1969) narrative conveys and as Jean Shinoda-Bolen (2001) suggests, different images of the divine feminine pertain to different aspects of the personality and to different stages in life. While involved in the research for this study and occupied with the writing process, the queen in the *Splendor Solis* has become an attractive image for me (see Henderson and Sherwood 2003, plate II-6). Donned in blue and gold, she represents the quintessence, a fifth stage that follows the *rubedo* (mentioned in relation to painting 3). In the picture, the queen is the center of a lively scene portraying the arts, sciences, and crafts in many forms. As Henderson and Sherwood write:

> This scene of city life and industry is a fitting representation of what we mean by the activities animated by the Logos principle. These activities involve tangible creativity: philosophy, the arts, and the sciences all governed by rational planning and discrimination. Here the

focus is not on interpersonal relating but upon an inner capacity for work, the performance of skilled tasks with joy and inspiration in a context ruled by a *principle* of discipline (often thought of as patriarchal in Western culture). (Ibid., p. 142)

This queen has the title of the Muse and is viewed as the creative feminine. In the picture, standing on a golden effigy of a man's face, she represents foremost the "personification of the creative man's anima." But the authors assert that "she can also serve as a symbol for anyone who is in the process of creating something of lasting value; the work itself is felt to come from a feminine source infused with eros" (ibid., p. 146). For my own purposes, I regard the queen as a quintessential personification of a woman who is undertaking an intellectual-spiritual study—an opus. The man's face she is standing on, then, is an image of Mercurius as her animus: transforming agent and the transformed. At the beginning of the work, Mercurius represented and was hidden in the *prima materia*, volatile and often a *cervus fugitivus*, trickster and malefic. At the end stage, his face is golden, for he has turned into a faithful servant or partner with whom the queen is in a conscious relationship. He even lets himself be used as a golden platform upon which she is standing.

At the end of my process, then, the image of the original, archaic goddess has differentiated into a complementary pair: the cat/priestess/goddess and the alchemical queen in the alembic. The former, linked to the Egyptian goddess Bastet and the Greek nature goddess Artemis, is an image of the wild woman archetype (Pinkola-Estes 1992). The latter relates to the Greek goddess Athena, associated with the arts, crafts, and intellectual endeavors. These two goddesses, moreover, are well suited to represent the two aspects contained in the etymology of the grail (according to Chevalier and Gheerbrant 1969, p. 178), namely as both *vessel* and *book*, "confirming the twofold meaning of what it contains—life and revelation."

Alchemical Painting:
A Method of Active Imagination

It was the memory of a childhood activity that furnished the necessary spark of inspiration: when I was growing up in Switzerland, children were shown how to create a symmetrical image using colorful paint blots on paper that was then folded, allowed to dry, and then pulled apart. The painted paper was used to bind books or wrap presents. Of course, no one associated the Rorschach inkblot test with this activity; the results were purely decorative.

My method, on the other hand, has an obvious connection to the test, as both are based on perception and an intuitive recognition of representational objects in the inkblot or paint blot. In that regard, McCully offers a profound observation in his study of the Rorschach test:

> The psyche itself may be something like an inkblot structure . . . .
> Both the substance of Rorschach's inkblots and the substance of
> the psyche itself provide the conditions which allow images to form
> around stimuli that are potent enough to precipitate them. Inkblots
> are as potent as their stimulus power. We are calling that power
> archetypal power. (Quoted in Spiegelman 1989, p. 198)

Rather than describing the utility of the Rorschach as a standardized diagnostic tool, McCully sees through to the archetypal foundation, the connection between psyche and inkblot, which I had grasped intuitively and played with. In the Rorschach test, the person is asked to give as many associations as possible for a given inkblot (without being expected to participate further), whereas my method is a way to engage in a dialogue, at times even a confrontation (*Auseinandersetzung*), with the living psyche. One stays with the first impression, working to fully know the image, trusting that this is how the soul wants to be personified and to make itself known on that given day.

In my method, the technique of creating the paint blot itself is an essential part of the procedure—the beginning of the meditative activity, of *serio ludere* (serious play). Much like the alchemists, I manipulate and observe the material—albeit here we have paint and paper instead of metals and minerals. Nonetheless, it is a method that combines substances and procedures (paint and the manipulation of the paper) in a close collaboration. There is a synchronous development between what happens with the substances and inner psychic states, as observed by the ego. While focusing with rapt attention and anticipation on what happens before me, I know that I am also attending to an inner process, according to the famous alchemical quote: "as within so without." Here, then, are the steps involved, in association with alchemical operations.

Step 1

In preparation for my active imagination, I settle in my specially designated place for meditation and contemplation. In my inner world I open up space through quieting or emptying the mind, while keeping the body still. I sit on the floor, the white paper before me. There is a distinct sense of entering a *temenos*. Being fully present awakens a heightened awareness and readiness to listen to psyche.

Wherever I settle for my meditation, it becomes a special place for the moment. Perhaps I have a designated spot, in front of a personal altar; perhaps I need to seek each time what feels right. Huxley notes that "to set boundary around a place, a person, or a state of mind is to set it apart, which is one of the customary definitions of the sacred" (1959, p. 11). The impulse to sacralize is part of human culture; it is the same all over the world. Jung calls the sacred space the *temenos*, a hallowed spot where the religious mysteries of transformation are performed (1952b, par. 171). Jung maintains that the *temenos* is of a feminine nature, symbolically associated with the womb, and often depicted as a secret garden (ibid., pars. 257 and 155). Jungian analysts and therapists think of their office space as a *temenos*, wherein the transformational processes of individuation are initiated.

138

For the alchemists, the laboratory was a *temenos*, and their work was an ongoing prayer. A respectable alchemist typically had two rooms for his work: the *laboratory*, where the experiments were carried out, and the *oratory*, for prayer. Because nowadays we often refer to the laboratory as the "lab," the word appears to encompass both activities, although it comes from the Latin, *laborare*, "to work." For the spiritual alchemist, prayer (*meditatio*) was an important part of the work. Meditation was understood as "an inner dialogue with God, . . . or with himself, or with his good angel" (Jung, quoting the alchemist Ruland, in 1952b, par. 390), that is, as a form of active imagination.

Step 2

I use a paper that is sturdy enough to be soaked with water but supple enough to be folded (a good-quality typing paper, for example). First, I moisten the whole paper with a big brush or a sponge. Then I fill the big brush with watercolor paint—one color, then another, according to my fancy, that is, my mood. Here I might splash randomly, there move the brush as in a slow dance, watching how the colors flow into each other. What I render on the paper is the image of chaos as I imagine it, a melting pot of the elements in an unformed state, reflected in flowing watercolors. Quite often tears are flowing as well.

This first stage corresponds to the alchemical operation of *solutio*, a dissolution and suspension in water, corresponding to one's inner world in a state of uncertainty and flux. Edinger quotes two texts: one says, "*solutio* is the root of alchemy"; the other advises, "until all be made water, perform no operation" (1985, p. 47). Edinger suggests this to mean "the return of differentiated matter to its original undifferentiated state—that is, to *prima materia*" (ibid.). Jung speaks to the metaphor of chaos and the struggle involved: "If a man puts his hand to the opus, he repeats, as the alchemists say, God's work of creation. The struggle with the unformed, with the chaos of Tiamat, is in truth a primordial experience" (1948b, par. 286). In a way, the process of creating one of my paint blots during the crisis situation was a contained reflection of the struggle with the "chaos of Tiamat," going on simultaneously in the external situation and on the inner psychic plane.

James Elkins, looking at oil painting from an alchemical perspective, maintains that for all practical matters one cannot really paint the chaos or *prima materia*, for "there is no such thing as absolute absence of structure, or pure randomness: if there were, we would be unable to perceive it at all" (2000, p. 94). Elkin notes that there are two basic choices for the *prima materia*: either it is a boiling mixture of all the elements of the world, or it is emptiness, like the calm sublime waters in the second verse of Genesis (1:25): "The earth was without form, and void; and darkness was upon the face of the deep." Alchemists, Elkins observes, "loved those words, 'without form and void'" (ibid., p. 84). In my method, the white paper would represent the void, whereas the merging watercolors represent the boiling elements or chaos. If one is depressed, the initial state is perhaps the most dangerous: one could get stuck staring listlessly at the white paper. But as soon as one lifts a hand and dips the brush into the water, there is life, energy; there is movement and the beginning of creating the *prima materia*, as it were, translating the initial mood into colors on the paper in a hermeneutical act.

I do not claim that a rectangular piece of paper is equivalent to the alchemical *vas hermeticum*, which had to be perfectly round "in imitation of the spherical cosmos" (Jung 1952b, par. 338). Yet the paper works well enough when keeping in mind that the vessel of the alchemists is not just the retort or flask. As Jung points out, it can also be "a mystical idea, a true symbol like all the central ideas of alchemy" (ibid.).

Step 3

The next step is the folding of the paper so that the wet paint is inside. I rub the two halves against each other with my fist, sometimes gently, sometimes more forcefully. There are a variety of ways of folding the paper: one can fold it only once (as in the Rorschach inkblot), creating a left and right or up and down symmetry. One can also experiment with two or more folds and irregular folds. One may even crumple the paper together in a ball, which gives the image an overall texture similar to a batik.

The chaos is now contained inside and under pressure from my hands. It is an intense moment, however subtle, to be rubbing the folded paper, perhaps planting my hand firmly onto it for a few seconds. I anticipate the paint coagulating into strange enigmatic forms and shapes.

I attribute this step to the *coagulatio* operation. In alchemy, it pertains to the element of earth. Cooling or drying turns liquids into solids. The stuff assumes a fixed, permanent shape or form. Edinger notes:

> Concepts and abstractions don't coagulate . . . . The images of dreams and active imagination do coagulate. They connect the outer world with the inner world . . . and thus coagulate soul-stuff. Moods and affects toss us about wildly until they coagulate into something visible and tangible; then we can relate to them objectively. (1985, p. 100)

140

We are reminded here of Jung's insistence that active imagination must be fixated (written down or given some creative expression) to make it real. In alchemy, it was the spirit Mercurius as elusive quicksilver that needed to be coagulated, meaning that the spirit had to be incarnated. It has to do with the flesh, and therefore with desire, says Edinger; consequently, "*desire coagulates*" (ibid., p. 87). In practice, he maintains, *coagulatio* is important for patients who have "an inadequate libido investment," a lack of desire that borders on anhedonia (ibid., p. 90). This, I would think, also describes the depressed state of someone who has experienced a loss of soul. What is awakened (or recovered) here could well be described with a phrase of the French philosopher Nabert, "the effort to exist and the desire to be" (quoted in Ricoeur 1981, p. 17). Through *coagulatio*, then, the soul comes back to the body. From that perspective, the very technique of manipulation described here is an example of soul-making.

Saturn and the moon (Luna) govern *coagulatio*, and the process is associated with the feminine principle. Edinger writes: "Any specific form, manifestation, or structure that solidifies our life energies into particular, concrete expression is of the nature of woman" (1985, pp. 96–97). Moreover, "*coagulatio* is often equated with creation" and is "promoted by action" (ibid., pp. 83, 85). In the cosmogony of the Native Americans, for example, the Earth is often created through the helpful action of an animal. Edinger also mentions a Hindu myth in which the world is created through churning and agitating motions. Indeed, at this stage in my process, there is action by manipulation—through folding, pressing, and rubbing the paper, accompanied by an inner movement that is created by the flow of energy.

Step 4

I let the paint dry, while sitting empty-minded in contemplation. Then I carefully unfold the paper, flatten it out, and lay the painting before me. I now behold the colorful forms and mysterious shapes, sometimes while turning the paper slowly in every direction to appreciate the product from all sides. This moment marks the height of suspension and curiosity: What is being revealed to me? Who wants to speak to me today? There is always surprise, whether delightful, awesome, or frightening, at the moment the other is personified and recognized. I might see the whole image at once or initially just a salient piece while the rest emerges during painting.

141

Here I look at the alchemical operation *separatio*. It is often the first step in creation stories, including Genesis. At this point in my process, there are various aspects of separation. Not only do I manipulate the paper by opening (separating) what has been folded, I also separate myself from the painting. In this very instance of laying it out before me, it becomes an "other," a Thou, that is its own being (McNiff 1992). If before I have been in a state of *participation mystique*, where the paint and paper and I and my actions were all intermingled, now the painting and I are two separate beings. "The elemental *separatio* that ushers in conscious existence is the separation of subject from object, the I from the not-I" says Edinger (1985, p. 187).

Step 5

Using a fine brush to follow and emphasize a shape here or fill out and enhance a form there, I give greater definition to the objects, figures, or scenery that my inner eye perceives. I obey a perceived necessity to transform the chaos into a world, making a considerable effort to work on the painting until there is a sense of completion. I bring out not what I want, but whatever is revealed to me. It entails repeated minute instances of surrender along the way. Each time the critic in my mind has an objection, the observing ego (guided by the wisdom of the Self) must intervene and put the critic in its place, encouraging the process to go on.

Active imagination honors the reality of the psyche. Like the alchemists, we work with the true and not with the fantastic imagination. At the time of painting my images, the latter would have imagined the illness gone and the crisis disappeared (a wish still strongly reflected in the first painting and poem). Imagination that works with the reality of the psyche induces true surrender and requires that we accept and work with what *is* (exemplified in the paintings that followed).

In an inner gesture of surrender, I suspend the critical, discriminating mind and accept whatever figures I perceive in the coagulated paint—the immediate, momentary reflection of the living, autochthonous psyche in response to outer circumstances and inner states (Romanyshyn 2000, p. 28). On another day, and for another person, something different would have emerged (as is true for me now, revisiting the work so many years later). The alchemist approaches his or her work with a "free and empty mind" in harmony with the work (Jung 1952b, par. 380). The text Jung quotes admonishes that "one must keep the eyes of the mind and soul well open, observing and contemplating by means of that inner light which God has fit in nature and in our hearts from the beginning" (ibid.).

Elkins notes, "from the artist's vantage, the moment when paint suddenly forms itself into something is always at stake—always vexed, always sudden and mysterious" (2000, p. 130). He likens it to the alchemical distillation, which is "the unpredictable, dangerous agitation that immediately precedes transcendence" (ibid.). The moment of recognition is indeed very special, whether for the oil painter who has worked brushstroke by brushstroke until suddenly the image becomes visible or the imaginal painter who recognizes the object that wants to be attended to in the coagulated forms of the paint before putting the brush to work.

Step 6

I end my painting effort with a deep sigh, prompted by the emotional release and the satisfaction that come after a concentrated effort. In an intense inner, silent dialogue with the image arisen from the unconscious, I have brought into being what I have not known before.

The symbolic content, as it touches me in the moment, speaks to me now. I listen and understand, but not with my analytical mind; rather, it is an understanding that comes from the heart and from a sense of wholeness. From that place, the words assemble themselves quite naturally into a poem, which seems to me to be the only suitable response.

At this stage, language is restored. I am still in meditation and still in the laboratory. The poem represents the first, completely intuitive, response to the image. Poetry is well suited for active imagination, eliciting further associations and metaphorical connections.

Step 7

I straighten myself and become more aware of my surroundings again; it is as if I have been in another world. I am in an altered state that often comes with meditation, but here there is the additional delight of the creation. This other world and the daily world, inner and outer, have become one. Pain, sorrow, and the feeling of loss have vanished for now; the great void experienced before as a dreadful emptiness is now filled with a transcendent love. There is the felt sense of a smiling presence in the room, or perhaps of benevolent presences. It is a numinous moment.

The feeling of oneness with the greater Self, with the world, the stars, the cosmos, and with one's fate describes the alchemical *coniunctio*. Edinger writes:

> That which goes by the name of love is fundamental to the phenomenology of the *coniunctio*. Love is both its cause and effect. The lesser *coniunctio* derives from love as concupiscence, whereas transpersonal love . . . both generates and is generated by the greater *coniunctio*. (1985, p. 223)

This one process is now complete. Each painting represents a process of active imagination in itself and has its own value. Because, in my particular situation at the time, there was no analyst supporting the endeavor, the psyche responded to and reflected back on the painting through life itself. The artwork was inextricably knitted into the fabric of life as it happened around me. Life in turn, responded to the daily meditations within the psychic field created, and this to and fro kept the momentum going for as long as it lasted.

Afterword and Acknowledgments

The journey that followed the events narrated here took a long and winding path, traversing a most varied psychic and physical terrain. As it turned out, Jürg underwent a second operation a year later, followed by a radical course of radiation. His last years as a handicapped person were in themselves an alchemical opus, transforming lead (a deep depression) into gold (the release of ego attachments and union with the Self) through his own kind of painting as a dialogue with the unconscious psyche. In part, this has been artfully chronicled in film by my brother-in-law, Christian Tauber, and a large collection of Jürg's delightful paintings are still awaiting publication.

After Jürg's passing, I found solace in therapy with Jungian analyst Elizabeth Bower, who later became a role model for embracing a career as therapist. Our work together will always hold a special place in my heart.

The master's program at the Professional School of Psychology in Sacramento, California, brought the first opportunity for me to present my series of paintings during Bill Berquist's seminar on intrusive life events in 1994. This awakened my desire to write the story and revisit our dream journals from the time of crisis. However, when my car, packed for a writer's retreat, was stolen, its contents, including the journals and the artwork, were lost. I deeply mourned the loss but then took it as a sign that the time to explore these earlier events had not come yet, and I counted myself lucky to have made good copies of the original paintings, poems, and various journal entries.

In the years that followed, I found my way to Pacifica Graduate Institute, where tending to the soul is at the center of academic research and of being in the world, and it felt like coming home. I am deeply indebted to the faculty members I met and worked with. Their broad vision and space for the imagination and the imaginal allowed me to work with my material as part of my dissertation. I am especially grateful to have had Dyane Sherwood as an exquisitely attuned advisor.

A predoctoral internship at the Jung Institute of San Francisco, private practice under the supervision and tutelage of Alan Ruskin, and analysis with Richard Stein provided fertile ground for professional learning and the deepening of personal growth. I cherish these experiences and hold fond memories of those years.

When the time was ripe to create this book, I felt ever so blessed that Murray Stein took an interest in the project. He has mentored it through its various stages with his finely honed sensibility for the expressions of psyche. Knowing that he has many engagements, I am humbled by his generosity of spirit and available presence at every stage. Siobhan Drummond, at Chiron Publications, has been a wonderful editor. Her expertise in producing books of art, her fine sense of style, and her attention to detail came to benefit every aspect of my work and made for a very enjoyable and fruitful collaboration.

My love goes to my children—Jonas, Maya, and Silvia—witnesses to my endeavors while pursuing their individual careers and founding their own families. I extend a heartfelt thank you for bearing with me through the years of school, training, and writing and for making yourselves available for questions concerning our shared past! I appreciated your valuable feedback and unabashed critique at every point of the writing process. My three grandchildren, on the other hand, with their infectious joie de vivre, have been the most delightful deterrent from desk and computer.

Finally, I want to express my gratitude to my precious friends and colleagues who have been companions on this winding path. Your interest in this book sustained and supported me, and your encouragement helped me when I lost faith. Without listing names, if you read this, know that I am thinking of you!

Notes

1 The expression "with the little eye of the soul" is found in several instances of Maier's works, including the *Hymnoso-phia*: "The phoenix is not only to be found in Egypt, but also in Europe, provided that we look around 'with the little eye of the soul'" (quoted by Tilton 2003, p. 76); and *De Philosophia Aegyptiorum*: "a knowl-edge of divine things . . . , which proceeds through the gnostic and revelatory opera-tion of 'the little eye of the soul'" (ibid., p. 241). Michael Maier (1568–1622), a true renaissance man—German physician, counselor to Rudolf II von Habsburg, phi-losopher, spiritual alchemist, poet, artist, and amateur composer—wrote a number of works, of which the *Atlanta fugiens* is perhaps his best known (referred to these days on the Internet as an early example of multimedia).

2 James Hillman introduced the term *soul-making* into depth psychology; he was fond of quoting Keats, who wrote in a letter: "Call the world, if you please, 'The vale of Soul-making.' Then you will find out the use of the world" (see, for example, Hillman 1992, p. xv).

3 An excellent introduction is Joan Chodorow's *Jung on Active Imagination* (1997), in which Jung's writings on the subject, scattered throughout his *Col-lected Works*, are comprehensively orga-nized. My own dissertation (Tauber 2005) includes an extensive literature review, to date. Most recently, Sherry Salman (2010) discusses active imagination from a radi-cal postmodern perspective.

4 Jung himself movingly describes how he came about the process in the chapter "Confrontation with the Unconscious" of his autobiography (1965). Now that we are in possession of his long-awaited *Red Book* (2009), his weighty magnum opus, we can appreciate his own testimony—profound dialogues with figures that arose spontaneously from the unconscious, superb illustrations, and mind-shatter-ing prophesies. Various conferences, seminars, and essays by Jungian analysts have since provided insight into this work.

Later Jungians have clarified and diversified the process, beginning with Marie-Louise von Franz (1978), who defined four distinct steps: 1) empty the ego mind; 2) let the unconscious flow into the vacuum; 3) add the ethical element (*Auseinandersetzung*, i.e., confrontation), as the ego reacts to the material; and 4) integrate the imagination, that is, draw conclusions and apply it to daily life. On the far end of this spectrum is D. Hartman (1999), who differentiated eighteen steps.

5 Jung's analogy between individuation, alchemy, and active imagination is stated, for example, in the following paragraph from *Psychology and Alchemy*:

> Alchemy set itself the task of acquir-ing this "treasure hard to attain" and of producing it in visible form, as the physical gold or the panacea or the transforming tincture—in so far as the art still busied itself in the laboratory. But since the practical, chemical work was never quite free from the uncon-scious contents of the operator which found expression in it, it was at the same time a psychic activity which can best be compared with what we call active imagination . . . . The process is in both cases an irrigation of the conscious mind by the unconscious,

and it is related so closely to the world of alchemical ideas that we are probably justified in assuming that alchemy deals with the same, or very similar, processes as those involved in active imagination and in dreams, that is, ultimately with the process of individuation. (1952b, par. 448.)

6 Elisabeth Tauber (or "Sabi" as she was called) had had a good part of her analysis with Jung, while also working with Barbara Hannah, between 1950 and 1961. She later studied astrology under the tutelage of Jung's daughter, Gret Baumann, and became a gifted astrologer herself. Ignaz Tauber, a general physician, underwent analysis with M.-L. von Franz and saw Jung a few times in private sessions. He later enjoyed many years as president of the Psychological Club in Zürich. Like the Wheelwrights, the couple maintained that Jung had "saved their marriage," that is, Jung's psychology had given them the tools they needed to negotiate their differences. They quickly became part of that first generation of Jungians (chronicled in Paul Stern's biography of Jung [1976, pp. 242–245]; Deidre Baer [2003] only mentions them in passing). Jung had taken a special liking to the family, visiting their home in Winterthur a number of times. The first time, they gathered around the fireplace for storytelling and a meal. Later, they held a few afternoon seminars for a small circle of physician friends (some of it recorded; see Tauber 1969). Sabi and Ignaz modeled a creative and dynamic example of applying Jung's psychology in daily life and tirelessly passed on his wisdom. Jung loomed large (indeed, sometimes too large) as a spiritual "Great Father," omnipresent, like the air we breathed.

7 Incidentally, this is the first of several instances in the poems where I refer to myself with a masculine connotation. It was an unexamined tradition in patriarchal Switzerland, where women, assuming spiritual or intellectual authority attributed to themselves the masculine pronoun.

8 Jung (1952b, chapter 3) notes that a central red ball, disk, or globe has the quality of a mandala, which he considers a foremost symbol of the Self.

9 Neumann writes: "The manipulation of these substances has formed part of the woman's primordial knowledge from her earliest dominion . . . . All these aids merely set in motion a natural potency of the female psyche, through which from time immemorial woman, in her character of shaman, sibyl, priestess, and wise woman, has influenced mankind" (1955, pp. 294–295).

10 Quoted from Jung 1932, par. 525. As it turns out, the original text in German does not have the definition ". . . of our own natures." The English translator, R. C. H. Hull, must have taken a liberty here, which, in my view, is restrictive and doesn't do justice to Jung's personal experience of a *mundus imaginalis* with psychic energies (in personified form) arising from beyond our inner-psychic boundaries.

11 At the time, reading such a text in its masculine form (especially in German, where "someone," *jemand,* has a masculine gender) fit right into my cosmology. Nowadays, after my own "feminist revision" (see Rowland 2002), I'm apt to read a text that accurately concerns me, or describes my situation, by changing the gendered articles and pronouns to reflect the feminine. The profound effect such an adapted reading has on me as a woman never fails to amaze me.

12 Here we have come upon the second incident where I refer to the woman in masculine gender: "the wise one" in my poem—so obviously a woman in the picture—is, in German, "the wise *man* in his secret dwelling" (*der Weise . . . in seiner Verborgenheit*). In this particular instance, it not only betrays my personal complex and the cultural implications of patriarchal language but also points to the history of Delphi. At the time I created this artwork, I would never have consciously doubted the superiority of the masculine and the men in my life, with respect to intellect and spiritual power, clarity, and wisdom. The extensive use of the I Ching in the Jungian circles early on, with its references to "the wise man" and "the noble man," had only deepened my respect. Paradoxically, the feminine counterpart, *die Weise*, would most likely be heard as *die Waise*, meaning an orphaned girl. Otherwise one would need to specify: *die weise Frau* (the wise woman). At any rate, this study offers me the opportunity to repair, from today's vantage point, the injustice I unwittingly did to myself. I want to acknowledge my wisdom in doing the work through which I received the daily ministrations of the soul. My free-form English translation of the poem reflects the change.

13 Carol Lee-Flinders (1998) argues poignantly how difficult it still is for contemporary women to reconcile a spiritual hunger and a feminist thirst, as the subtitle of her book indicates. She identifies a number of precepts with regard to meditative practices that are constants, whether broadly or narrowly interpreted. These are: 1) to be silent, 2) to put oneself last, 3) to resist and rechannel one's desires, and 4) to enclose oneself. These precepts, Lee-Flinders maintains, "cancel the basic freedoms—to say what one wants, go where one likes, enjoy whatever pleasures one can afford, and most of all, to be somebody—that have normally defined male privilege" (p. 84). For men, they entail "a dramatic and painful reversal of status; hopefully, an all-out assault on the male ego" (p. 84). Women, on the other hand, "have not been in a position to renounce these privileges voluntarily *because they never had them in the first place*" (ibid., emphasis in the original). In fact, the author says, these precepts look suspiciously close to the counseling young brides receive in traditional cultures and are still, in veiled forms or under tacit threats, mandates for our girls approaching womanhood. "These are the terms of our subordination" (p. 85), Lee-Flinders points out, which contemporary feminism vigorously repudiates, urging women quite in contrast to find their voices, know who they are, reclaim their bodies, and move about freely and fearlessly!

14 See, for example, Wolkstein and Kramer, *Inanna: Queen of Heaven and Earth* (1983); Perera, *Descent to the Goddess: A Way of Initiation for Women* (1981); and Meador, *Uncursing the Dark: Treasures from the Underworld* (1994).

15 A theme to which Stanton Marlan (2005) has dedicated pages of sophisticated philosophical discussion.

16 Like all archaic goddesses, the cat goddess had a sexual aspect, as part-cat quite naturally so. Even today, searching for an image of Bastet online inadvertently leads to soft pornography.

17 Jung notes that we are lacking an original text by a female alchemist (no manuscript by Maria herself has been preserved), and thus "we do not know what kind of alchemical symbolism a woman's view would have produced" (1946, par. 518), but his conjecture certainly strikes a chord!

References

Abraham, L. 1998. *A Dictionary of Alchemical Imagery*. Cambridge, UK: Cambridge University Press.

Austen, H. 1990. *The Heart of the Goddess: Art, Myth and Meditations of the World's Sacred Feminine*. Berkeley, CA: Wingbow Press.

Baer, D. 2003. *Jung: A Biography*. Boston: Little, Brown.

Becker, U. 1992. *The Continuum Encyclopedia of Symbols*. New York: Continuum, 2000.

Biedermann, H. 1989. *Dictionary of Symbolism: Cultural Icons and the Meaning Behind Them*. New York: Chevalier and Gheerbrant Books, 1994.

Bly, R. 1990. *Iron John: A Book about Men*. Menlo Park, CA: Addison-Wesley Publishing.

Chevalier, J., and A. Gheerbrant. 1969. *The Chevalier and Gheerbrant Dictionary of Symbols.* Translated by J. Buchanan-Brown. London: Author, 1994.

Chodorow, J., ed. 1997. *Jung on Active Imagination*. Princeton, NJ: Princeton University Press.

Coleman, A. 1997. "Pain and Surgery: The Shamanic Experience." In D. Sandner and S. Wong, eds., *The Sacred Heritage: The Influence of Shamanism on Analytical Psychology* (pp. 125–137). London: Routledge.

Cooper, J. C. 1978. *An Illustrated Encyclopaedia of Traditional Symbols*. London: Thames and Hudson.

Craze, R. 1969. *Hell*. Berkeley, CA: Conari Press, 1996.

Damery, P. 2004. "The Horned God: A Personal Discovery of Cultural Myth." *The San Francisco Jung Institute Library Journal* 23(3):7–28.

Douglas, C. 1990. *The Woman in the Mirror: Analytical Psychology and the Feminine*. Boston: Sigo Press.

Downing, C. 1969. *The Goddess: Mythological Images of the Feminine*. New York: Continuum, 1996.

Edinger, E. 1972. *Ego and Archetype*. New York: Chevalier and Gheerbrant.

———. 1985. *Anatomy of the Psyche: Alchemical Symbolism in Psychotherapy.* La Salle, IL: Open Court.

———. 1990. *The Living Psyche: A Jungian Analysis in Pictures*. Wilmette, IL: Chiron Publications.

Elkins, J. 2000. *What Painting Is*. New York: Routledge.

Flanagan, S. 1989. *Hildegard of Bingen: A Visionary Life*. London: Routledge.

Gimbutas, M. 1989. *The Language of the Goddess*. San Francisco: Harper.

Goodchild, V. 2001. *Eros and Chaos*. York Beach, ME: Nicolas-Hays.

Harding, E. 1935. *Women's Mysteries, Ancient and Modern*. New York: Harper and Row, 1971.

Hartman, D. 1999. "A Phenomenological Study of the Procedure of Active Imagination and Active Imagination as a Form of Western Imaginal or Visionary Meditation." PhD diss., Saybrook Institute. UMI Dissertation Services.

Henderson, J. 1983. "Ancient Myths and Modern Man." In C. G. Jung, ed., *Man and His Symbols* (pp. 104–157). Garden City, NY: Doubleday.

Henderson, J., and D. Sherwood. 2003. *Transformation of the Psyche: The Symbolic Alchemy of the Splendor Solis*. New York: Brunner-Routledge.

Hillman, J. 1980. "The Therapeutic Value of Alchemical Language." In I. F. Baker, ed., *Methods of Treatment in Analytical Psychology* (pp. 118–126). Seventh International Congress of the International Association for Analytical Psychology. Fellbach, Germany: Adolf Bonz.

——. 1983. *The Healing Fiction.* Barrytown, NY: Station Hill Press.

——. 1992. *Re-visioning Psychology.* New York: Harper and Row.

——. 2010. "Alchemical Blue and the Unio Mentalis." In *Alchemical Psychology,* uniform edition, vol. 5 (pp. 97–124). New York: Spring Publications.

Husain, S. 1997. *The Goddess.* Boston: Little, Brown.

Huxley, F. 1959. *The Way of the Sacred.* Garden City, NY: Doubleday, 1974.

Jung, C. G. 1932. "Psychotherapists or the Clergy." In *CW*, vol. 11. Princeton, NJ: Princeton University Press, 1969.

——. 1934. "The Practical Use of Dream-Analysis." In *CW*, vol. 16. Princeton, NJ: Princeton University Press, 1966.

——. 1935. *The Tavistock Lectures.* In *CW*, vol. 18. Princeton, NJ: Princeton University Press, 1976.

——. 1936. "Wotan." In *CW*, vol. 10. Princeton, NJ: Princeton University Press, 1964.

——. 1939–41. *Visions: Notes of the Seminar Given in 1930–1934*, 2 vols. Edited by C. Douglas. Princeton, NJ: Princeton University Press, 1997.

——. 1940. "Psychology and Religion." In *CW*, vol. 11. Princeton, NJ: Princeton University Press, 1969.

——. 1942. "Paracelsus as a Spiritual Phenomenon." In *CW*, vol. 13. Princeton, NJ: Princeton University Press, 1967.

——. 1946. "The Psychology of the Transference." In *CW*, vol. 16. Princeton, NJ: Princeton University Press, 1966.

——. 1948a. "A Review of the Complex Theory." In *CW*, vol. 8. Princeton, NJ: Princeton University Press, 1969.

——. 1948b. "The Spirit Mercurius." In *CW*, vol. 13. Princeton, NJ: Princeton University Press, 1967.

——. 1951. *Aion: Researches into the Phenomenology of the Self. CW*, vol. 9ii. Princeton, NJ: Princeton University Press, 1959.

——.1952a. "Foreword to Werblowsky's *Lucifer and Prometheus*." In *CW*, vol. 11. Princeton, NJ: Princeton University Press, 1969.

——. 1952b. *Psychology and Alchemy. CW*, vol. 12. Princeton, NJ: Princeton University Press, 1953.

——. 1952c. *Symbols of Transformation. CW*, vol. 5. Princeton, NJ: Princeton University Press, 1956.

——. 1954a. "On the Nature of the Psyche." In *CW*, vol. 8. Princeton, NJ: Princeton University Press, 1969.

——. 1954b. "The Philosophical Tree." In *CW*, vol. 13. Princeton, NJ: Princeton University Press, 1967.

——. 1954c. "Transformation Symbolism in the Mass." In *CW*, vol. 11. Princeton, NJ: Princeton University Press, 1969.

——. 1955–56. *Mysterium Coniunctionis. CW*, vol. 14. Princeton, NJ: Princeton University Press, 1970.

——. 1957. "Commentary on 'The Secret of the Golden Flower.' In *CW*, vol. 13. Princeton, NJ: Princeton University Press, 1967.

——. 1958. "Schizophrenia." In *CW*, vol. 3. Princeton, NJ: Princeton University Press, 1960.

——. 1965. *Memories, Dreams, Reflections.* Edited by A. Jaffé. New York: Vintage Books.

——. 2009. *The Red Book.* Edited by S. Shamdasani. New York: W. W. Norton.

Jung, C. G., and C. Kerenyi. 1949. *Essays on a Science of Mythology: The Myth of the Divine Child and the Mysteries of Eleusis.* Translated by R. F. C. Hull. Princeton, NJ: Princeton University Press, 1963.

152

Lee-Flinders, C. 1998. *At the Root of This Longing: Reconciling a Spiritual Hunger and a Feminist Thirst*. San Francisco: HarperSanFrancisco.

Littleton, S., ed. 2002. *The Illustrated Anthology of World Myth and Storytelling*. London: Duncan Baird Publishers.

Luke, H. 1995. *The Way of Woman: Awakening the Perennial Feminine*. New York: Doubleday.

Manheim, R. 1967. *Myth, Religion, and Mother Right: Selected Writings by J. J. Bachofen*. Princeton, NJ: Princeton University Press.

Marlan, S. 2005. *The Black Sun: The Alchemy and Art of Darkness*. College Station: Texas A & M University Press.

Matthews, B., trans. 1978. *The Herder Symbol Dictionary: Symbols from Art, Archaeology, Mythology, Literature, and Religion*. Wilmette, IL: Chiron Publications, 1987.

McNiff, S. 1992. *Art as Medicine*. Boston: Shambhala.

Meador, B. 1994. *Uncursing the Dark: Treasures from the Underworld*. Wilmette, IL: Chiron Publications.

Neumann, E. 1955. *The Great Mother: An Analysis of the Archetype*. Translated by R. Manheim. Princeton, NJ: Princeton University Press, 1991.

Noel, D. 2002. "Who Is the Green Man? An Ancient Pagan Icon Offers Visions of a Time We Cannot Remember." Accessed April 4, 2011, www.mythinglinks. org/ct~greenmen~DanNoel.html. (Reprinted from the *Santa Barbara Independent*, June 13–20, pp. 25–26).

Perera, S. B. 1981. *Descent to the Goddess: A Way of Initiation for Women*. Toronto: Inner City Books.

Pinkola-Estes, C. 1992. *Women Who Run with the Wolves*. New York: Ballantine Books.

Ricoeur, P. 1981. *Hermeneutics and the Social Sciences*. Edited and translated by J. Thompson. Cambridge, UK: Cambridge University Press, 1998.

Roberts, G. 1994. *The Mirror of Alchemy*. Toronto: University of Toronto Press.

Romanyshyn, R. 2000. "Alchemy and the Subtle Body of Metaphor: Soul and Cosmos." In R. Brooke, ed., *Pathways into the Jungian World* (pp. 27–47). London: Routledge.

Ronnberg, A. and K. Martin, eds. 2010. *The Book of Symbols*. Cologne, Germany: Taschen.

Rowland, S. 2002. *Jung: A Feminist Revision*. Cambridge, UK: Polity Press.

Salman, S. 1986. "The Horned God: Masculine Dynamics of Power and Soul." *Quadrant* 19(2):7–25.

———. 2010. "Peregrinations of Active Imagination: The Elusive Quintessence in the Postmodern Labyrinth." In M. Stein, ed., *Jungian Psychoanalysis* (pp. 118–133). La Salle, IL: Open Court.

Sams, J., and D. Carson. 1988. *Medicine Cards: The Discovery of Power through the Ways of Animals*. Santa Fe, NM: Bear and Company.

Schärf-Kluger, R. 1995. *Psyche in Scripture: The Idea of the Chosen People and Other Essays*. Toronto: Inner City Books.

Sherwood, D. 1997. "Cancer, New Age Guilt, and the Dark Feminine." In D. Sandner and S. Wong, eds., *The Sacred Heritage: The Influence of Shamanism on Analytical Psychology* (pp. 139–156). New York: Routledge.

Shinoda-Bolen, J. 2001. *Goddesses in Older Women: Archetypes in Women over 50*. New York: HarperCollins.

Skafte, D. 1997. *Listening to the Oracle*. San Francisco: HarperSanFrancisco.

Spiegelman, J. 1989. "Review of *Jung and Rorschach: A Study in the Archetype of Perception*." *Psychological Perspectives* 20(1):198–202.

Stern, P. 1976. *C. G. Jung: The Haunted Prophet*. New York: George Braziller.

Tauber, C., ed. 1969. *Winterthurer Fragestunden: C. G. Jung, über Gefühle und den Schatten* [Question and Answer Sessions in Winterthur: C. G. Jung on Feelings and the Shadow]. Compact disc. Zürich: Walter Verlag, 1996.

Tauber, M. 2005. "The Soul's Ministrations: Active Imagination as a Transformative Tool in Crisis." PhD diss., Pacifica Graduate Institute. UMI Dissertation Services.

Tilton, H. 2003. *Quest for the Phoenix: Spiritual Alchemy and Rosicrucianism in the Work of Count Michael Maier (1569–1622) (Arbeiten zur Kirchengeschichte)*. Berlin: Walter de Gruyter.

von Franz, M.-L. 1978. "On Active Imagination." In J. Baker, ed., *Methods of Treatment in Analytical Psychology* (pp. 88–99). Fellbach: Adolf Bonz Verlag, 1980.

——. 1997. *Alchemical Active Imagination*. Boston: Shambhala.

——. 1999. *The Cat: A Tale of Female Redemption*. Toronto: Inner City Books.

Walker, B. 1983. *The Women's Encyclopedia of Myths and Secrets*. San Francisco: Harper.

Watkins, M. 1984. *Waking Dreams*. Dallas: Spring Publications.

Whitmont, E. 1997. *Return of the Goddess*. New York: Continuum.

Wilber, K. 2000. *Grace and Grit*. Boston: Shambhala.

Wolkstein, D., and S. Kramer. 1983. *Inanna: Queen of Heaven and Earth*. New York: Harper and Row.

Woodman, M., and E. Dickson. 1969. *Dancing in the Flames: The Dark Goddess in the Transformation of Consciousness*. Boston: Shambhala, 1996.

Index

Gimbutas, Marija, 3, 70, 82–83, 103, 119, 121
goddess archetype, 3–4, 130–31
goddesses: cat priestess, 133–36; cow, 78–79; eye, 82; fish, 99, 119; love, 102, 134; moon, 82, 84, 86, 95, 116; owl, 82; tree, 88; triple, 87, 95; of the underworld, 110
grail (Holy Grail), 69, 128–29, 136
Great Goddess, 70, 79, 82–83, 86, 102–3
Great Mother, 78, 87–88, 94, 99, 106, 108, 116–17, 120, 133
Green Man, 91, 93
Gundestrup cauldron, 71

Hannah, Barbara, 147n6
Harding, Esther, 4, 107
Hartman, D., 146n4
Hathor, 78–79
Hecate, 82, 86, 95
hell, 87
Henderson, Jim, 4, 84, 97, 104, 118, 126, 130, 135
hero myth, 84
Herodotus, 131–32
Hildegard of Bingen, 127
Hillman, James, 4, 79–80, 103, 110, 130, 146n2
Hinduism, veils of Maya, 69
Hippocrates, 116
Horned God, 70–72, 83, 108, 117, 133
Huxley, F., 138

illness, as a sign of spiritual failing, 87
Inanna, 103, 108, 110–11, 114
incense, 100–1
individuation, 2, 4, 75, 85, 91, 96, 133, 135, 146n5
inflation, 122, 126
Irish mythology, 112–13
Ishtar, 69, 102, 134
Isis, 69, 78, 113
Ixchel, 84

Jenks, Kathleen, 91
Jesus, Oxyrhynchus sayings, 121
Jonah, and the whale, 120–21
Jung, C. G., 82; active imagination, 2, 4, 140; on alchemy, 73, 92, 100–2, 114, 124–25, 129, 135, 139, 142, 148n17; child archetype, 94, 96; on astrological symbolism, 116, 120–21; Christian symbolism, 106, 120; on complexes, 74; diamond body, 88, 90; on flower symbolism, 90–91; on nightmares, 95; on Paracelsus, 111; personal experience of a *mundus imaginalis*, 147n10; *Red Book*, 146n4; on Satan, 75; symbolism of the hen, 127; on *temenos*, 138; on Wotan, 127

Keats, John, 146n2
Kerenyi, Carl, 94

Lee-Flinders, Carol, 148n13
Lilith, 82, 114, 120
Lughnasadh, 71
Luke, Helen, 131–32

magic, 70
Maier, Michael, 1, 146n1
mandala, as a symbol of the Self, 147n8
Marlan, Stanton, 4, 110, 148n15
McNiff, Shaun, 1, 72
meditation, 72, 85; as a form of active imagination, 138
Mercurius (Mercury), 71, 75–76, 84, 89, 93, 96, 108, 114, 118, 134–136, 140
Milton, John, *Paradise Lost*, 75
moon god, 107–108

Native American mythology, 83, 113
Neumann, Erich, 4, 69–70, 78, 84, 86–87, 91, 102, 106–7, 133, 147n9
Noel, Dan, 91, 93

Osiris, 107